Survive the Drive

Dedications

I have been extremely fortunate. I have a great and supportive family that appears in numerous stories within these pages. I have wonderful friends who are like family, great colleagues and mentors who are some of my best friends, and students who have been my best teachers. The greatest part, though, is that most of them—and, certainly, all of the ones who appear in this book—fall in at least two of those categories. We have been on a long journey together, sometimes deliberate and sometimes random, and that journey has allowed us to do a great thing: Save people from needless injury and death from car crashes. How could a life and a life's work be any better than that?

-Tom Dingus

I owe thanks to some: family, friends, colleagues. They know who they are.

While the stories in this book are not mine, I am there in the sentence structure, the syntax, the re-writes. The way it was edited is representative of my thought process. Even the font selection. That's because I was fortunate enough to have a liberal arts education. Then I found a work community that saw the merit of intertwining a liberal arts mind with those of engineers. We took a chance on each other, and it worked. So I also owe thanks to my alma mater, Emory & Henry College, for fostering the liberal arts thinkers and doers. For pushing us to think in the gray, to see beyond black and white/ this or that. For helping us find a voice and to question. If you have a mathematician's mind, or an engineer's reason, the world needs that. But if you have a liberal arts mind—for writing, for the arts, for the creative—take a chance on that, because the world needs that logic just as much.

-Mindy Buchanan-King

Foreword

Consider the following:

- 90% of drivers in the U.S. think their driving performance is above average. That means at least 40% of drivers in the U.S. are overconfident in their abilities, and we should learn to watch out for them, particularly if "them" is "us."
- 10% of drivers in the U.S. create between 40% and 50% of the crash risk; we should really learn to look out for them. Definitely if "them" is "us."

These two simple facts should tell you something: Regardless of whether you fall into one or both categories or you are looking out for those who fall into one or both categories, we can all learn something about how best to avoid being in—or at least surviving—one of the 11 million crashes that occur in the U.S. every year. You will hopefully learn from this book that everyone, from new drivers to those who have been driving before seat belts were even a safety option, can improve their odds of surviving the dangers of driving by following a handful of tips that can make a big difference.

About *Survive the Drive*

Driving is risky business. Only cancer, heart attacks, and strokes rank higher in terms of the number of unintentional deaths occurring among the general population. Driving is the leading cause of unintentional death for those between the ages of 4 and 34.

Unlike cancer, heart attacks, and strokes, driving does not discriminate by age. More than 30,000 deaths and 2.5 million emergency room visits occur each year from crashes on U.S. highways alone. Many of these crash victims are teenagers or young adults, according to the National Highway Traffic Safety Administration (NHTSA) Fatality Analysis Reporting System. This system is commonly referred to in our industry as the FARS. In fact, all you have to do is look at the 2012 FARS Quick Facts sheet for a sobering reminder of the risks drivers face, from 6,454 injuries per day to 8,364 fatalities due to alcohol-impaired driving.

Maybe, relatively speaking, the risk of experiencing a fatal or disabling crash looks pretty low. After all, there are more than 300 million other people in the U.S. alone, 210 million of whom are licensed drivers. Let's put your crash risk into perspective, though: By far, more people die from driving than any of the other relatively "dangerous" activities shown below. The rate means the statistics below have been corrected by the number of participants. Let's take whitewater kayaking, for example. Out of 100,000 folks who kayak, an average of 2.9 people die in a given year while kayaking.

Fatality rate, per 100,000 participants

Whitewater kayaking	2.9
Climbing: Ice, snow, or rock	3.2
Recreational boating	6.5
Hunting	0.7
Skiing/snowboarding	0.4
Scuba diving	3.5
Driving	**15.2**

As you can see, you are much more likely to die in a car crash than you are to die participating in any of the other activities that may be characterized as "extreme" or "risky." What this illustrates is that our perception of risk is not very accurate. If you can understand the real risk of various activities, and how to reduce that risk, you can increase your odds of survival a great deal.

Driving is a risky activity that most everyone performs. For many, driving is an unavoidable part of life. So, why are you reading this? Simply put, this book will give you some tips about how to reduce your risk while behind the wheel. This book can't guarantee that all risks will be eliminated, but that's life!

Understanding Your Risk:
An Easy Math Lesson

This book tells you how to reduce your risk while behind the wheel by giving you estimates of the risk, or odds, associated with certain aspects of driving. Those aspects can range from distraction (think texting) to driving under the influence of alcohol.

The odds of something happening is a very simple concept to understand. Here, the odds will simply tell you how much more, or less, at risk you are compared to (most often) the ideal conditions of driving on dry roads in daylight while alert, attentive, and non-impaired. Where that comparison is not the case, I will let you know. Therefore, an odds of 1.0 means that you have exactly the same risk, doing whatever it is you are doing, as driving under the ideal circumstances described above. If the odds are twice as high, meaning they are at 2.0, then you are twice as likely to crash compared to driving under the ideal conditions. If the odds are 1.3, you are about 30% more likely to crash; if the odds are 6.0, then you are six times, or 600%, more likely to get in a crash versus driving under the ideal conditions.

I bring up this point because people, including the media, get percentages and odds confused. For example, the Virginia Tech Transportation Institute (VTTI), of which I am director, did an analysis that showed texting and driving for heavy-truck drivers increased the risk of a safety-critical event (meaning a crash, near-crash, minor collision, etc.) by 23 times. Unfortunately, some media sources then erroneously reported that "texting while driving increases your risk by 23%." That is a HUGE difference between our study results and what was reported. What got lost in the translation is: 1) The "23 times statistic" applies to heavy trucks, not to all vehicles; and 2) The increased crash risk in terms of percentages is not 23%, it is 2,300%!

Sometimes throughout this book, I have to use percentages to explain the risk because I don't have strong enough data to calculate the odds. For example, you need numbers like how many people didn't crash while driving on icy roads to calculate the odds of crashing on ice, which is sometimes hard to pinpoint. Therefore, you will see statements such as "increases fatal crash risk by 60%..." Just remember that this number is not exactly the same as an odds of 1.6. In general terms, though, the two convey roughly the same amount of risk.

There are times that the odds can be less than 1.0. In these cases, there exists what we refer to as a "protective effect." In other words, you have reduced your odds of a crash. A great example is the presence of passengers. If you are an adult (we will talk about teens later), the odds of you having a crash are about 0.5 when you are traveling with passengers relative to when you drive alone. Therefore, as an adult, you are twice as safe when passengers are present. We are not exactly sure why there is a reduced risk of a crash in this scenario, but there are certainly a few factors at play. First, adults tend to drive more conservatively when passengers are present. Second, passengers probably help keep the driver alert. And third, the passengers serve as "another set of eyes" to spot hazards. My wife, Melissa, is a very good "crash avoidance system" in this regard, letting me know in no uncertain terms when I have missed or underestimated a potential hazard.

The risk of a crash will be characterized throughout this book by my best guess at the odds or percentages. My "best guess" means that sometimes the risk is scientifically well established, while other times it is based on my expertise gained from more than 30 years of research experience in the field. Most of the time, there are scientific papers or reports to back up the risk odds or percentages, either written by myself or with co-authors, or by esteemed colleagues in the field. Therefore, each chapter of this book includes a general resources section should you want to delve into the scientific details. Within this book, I am providing odds and percentage estimates so that you can understand the crash risks and decide accordingly how best to reduce your personal odds and that of your kids, parents, friends, and/or spouse. Hopefully, you will follow many of the tips in this book so your odds of suffering a serious crash will be less than half compared to your risk before you read the book.

The Data Used

The odds and percentages provided in each section are almost exclusively based on studies conducted in actual field settings or from databases derived from actual crashes. While laboratory and/ or simulation studies have benefits, our ability to estimate crash risk from such closed environments is limited as of this writing.

There are several large crash databases that are developed and stored by the National Highway Traffic Safety Administration (NHTSA). The sources of these data are primarily police reports filled out by investigating officers after a crash. Other databases are developed through more in-depth analyses conducted by trained crash investigators. These databases are powerful tools that help us understand much about crash factors, and they are referenced throughout this book.

What is very hard, or sometimes even impossible, to gauge using post-crash investigations is what happened in the seconds leading up to a crash. This timeframe is critical for determining such factors as driver drowsiness, distraction, error, aggressive driving, or road conditions. Crash investigation reports are only as good as the information collected by the investigator, and the majority of that information comes from interviewing those involved in the crash. However, following a crash, drivers and/or passengers may be dead, injured, are always dazed, may not have been looking in the right direction, may not remember what occurred, or may be trying to hide something. That is why the naturalistic driving study research method was developed.

The naturalistic driving study research method was pioneered 20 years ago by the Virginia Tech Transportation Institute (VTTI) and has been fine-tuned since that time. In the late 1990s, I began collaborating with a friend and colleague named Mike Goodman. Mike was from NHTSA (there is a photo of him later in the book). Together, we worked on what would become the first large-scale naturalistic driving study. The study used 100 cars traveling on the road for 13 months. A brilliant team of VTTI hardware and software engineers and fellow researchers helped us create and define the concept behind naturalistic driving studies. We determined we needed more real-world data to explain why people crashed. We needed data from the vehicles themselves to determine what was happening at the time of what we call a safety-critical event, meaning a crash, near-crash, minor collision, etc. We also needed video to corroborate what was happening with the vehicle. For instance, if the car experienced a sudden deceleration, we needed visuals to determine why the driver slammed on the brakes. Was the driver distracted? Fatigued? Impaired?

Example screenshot from naturalistic driving video; photo courtesy of VTTI

The instrumentation for undertaking naturalistic driving studies includes an inconspicuous suite of cameras, sensors, and radar. Only volunteers are used for these studies; they receive no training and no directions from VTTI researchers. The only task of these participants is to drive as they normally do. For nearly two decades, we have equipped more than 4,000 vehicles to collect what now stands at more than one million hours of continuous naturalistic driving data. We have also captured more than 1,500 crashes (and counting) and more than 10,000 near-crashes as part of this data collection effort. This unique data resource is continually tapped by federal transportation agencies, departments of transportation, even major automobile manufacturers. It is the cornerstone of our primary goal at VTTI: To save lives.

It's No Accident

Throughout this book, you will never see use of the word "accident." Well, technically, you'll never see it used after this paragraph. I used to charge students in my transportation safety class 25 cents every time they used the word "accident." By the end of the semester, we had enough money for pizza. Why did I put them through this? Because "accident" implies an unfortunate event that can't be controlled or managed; an accident is something that just happens. As you will read in this book, however, you have significant control over your risk while driving. If these risks are properly managed, you can avoid many, many crashes. You also have the capability to manage the potential consequences for those cases during which a crash cannot be avoided. For instance, you can choose a safe vehicle, wear personal protective gear that includes a seat belt, or wear a bicycle or motorcycle helmet if you are of the two- or three-wheel crowd. All of these choices affect how a crash will impact your life.

So, read on and learn how to best control your driving situation, manage your risk, and avoid or lessen the probability or severity of a CRASH!

But, keep in mind that crashes do happen. About 11 million per year in the United States. Even if you do everything right, you may get in a crash. Therefore, it is just as important to make sure that, if someone crashes into you, you have done everything you can to not only survive, but to walk away.

How a Crash is Like Baking a Cake

Most of today's information is distilled down into a single sound bite, a lone fact that has virtually no context. This seems to be particularly true when it comes to driving safety. You often hear news reports that claim one cause for a crash, such as "A driver, under the influence of alcohol, hit a cyclist…" However, crashes themselves—and the degree to which those involved are injured—are rarely the result of a single factor. Inevitably, there are contributing factors at play: The driver may have been dialing a phone, the crash may have occurred at night, the cyclist may have been wearing dark clothing with minimal or no reflectors, and the driver may have actually had a blood alcohol content below the legal limit. These multiple factors are known as the interaction between causal (primary) and contributing (secondary) factors.

One thing that you will notice as you read this book is, if you add up all of the percentages of crash risk factors (such as alcohol, inattentive driving, aggressive driving, drowsy driving), you will be way over 100%. You may ask "How can this be?" It's because three or four factors often interact to cause a single crash.

One can think about this phenomenon like a recipe—let's say it's a recipe for a birthday cake, given the title of this section. Each ingredient in this figurative birthday cake represents a factor that can contribute to a crash. A crash itself happens when the ingredients are present to complete the "mix." Sometimes, the factor is such that you are primed to experience a crash (say, the eggs in the cake).

Sometimes, the factor is not present, so the cake is never made. An example is taking your eyes off of the road to glance at something. Distraction becomes the key ingredient in this scenario. But, if one or more other ingredients aren't present—say, the car in front of you doesn't brake unexpectedly while you are distracted—then a crash won't occur. It's when you have three or four factors working against you while driving that you typically have a crash. Therefore, one way to think about how to avoid crashes is to make sure there is a figurative key ingredient that you keep out of the cake recipe.

In addition to the crash causal and contributing factors, there are other ingredients that determine whether you are injured and to what extent. Let's think of these ingredients as the proverbial icing on the cake. These ingredients include such factors as how well your vehicle is designed to protect you during a crash (also known as crashworthiness); whether or not you are wearing a seat belt; and/or the presence of heavy, loose objects in the vehicle that could become dangerous projectiles during a crash.

The following is an example from my own history to illustrate this recipe simile.

My friend, Rick, left our home in Fairborn, Ohio, after graduating from Wright State University (it was the "wright" place to be...) to attend graduate school at the University of Illinois. During Rick's semester break, our friend named Bob, (another) Rick, and I hopped into my 1973 VW Bus and headed bravely across Indiana to check out this town in Illinois. How can you go wrong when your college buddy moves to a town called "Champagne"?

As we were known to do, we had a spirited weekend. However, something called "The Blizzard of '78" was happening right outside our door. We were having a grand time, barely noticing the blizzard. We even managed to dig out and buy six cases of beer and a few bottles of liquor to take back home because it was cheaper to buy in Illinois.

When the end of the weekend arrived, we headed east at a snail's pace due to the weather. Since the heater was so terrible in my bus, Bob brought along a portable propane heater. Rick was sitting cross-legged with his shoes off. Of course, the beer and liquor we purchased was just sitting in the back of the VW bus (unopened, obviously) since there was no trunk. As we traveled along, out of Illinois and into Indiana, the road conditions slowly improved. Our speed gradually crept from 25 mph, to 35 mph, to 45 mph, all the way to 55 mph because the roads were plowed and salted. I was in a hurry to get home because I had an upcoming week filled with several tests and needed to study. We were feeling really good about the trip back home…until we passed under an overpass that also happened to be a county line. Turns out the roads in Indiana were maintained by county. Unfortunately, the county into which we had crossed had not yet extended its road maintenance onto I-70.

As we crossed "the line," the interstate was sheer ice. Cars were scattered everywhere in both ditches. Our VW bus didn't fare any better. We started spinning out and spun around backwards. My friend Rick said the most intelligent thing I had heard in a while: "Hold on!" We hit the median, and the bus rolled over 1.75 times. I had a death grip on the steering wheel because we didn't have seat belts on. I distinctly remember the windshield popping out on the first rollover. Bob wrestled a time or two with his heater.

When it was all over, my bus looked like an A-frame. There were broken beer bottles everywhere, and we were soaked in beer. It was 20 degrees outside. Rick had a chipped tooth and never found his shoes. Bob had a cut over his eye, but that was (thankfully) the extent of the bodily damage incurred. No one was cut from all of the broken glass. There was one unbroken bottle, a fifth of Jack Daniels, which had flown through the windshield between Rick and me, landing about 20 feet in front of the bus. Cars had already pulled over going the opposite way, and a state patrolman followed within a minute.

We grabbed our duffle bags. I talked to the patrolman, who was very sympathetic even though I was soaked in beer because it was 9:30 a.m. and he had probably received 20 calls within 20 minutes about other crashes on the interstate. I filled out the paperwork, the officer called a tow truck, and he gave us a ride to the Greyhound bus station. We had a couple of hours to wait for our bus. It was a surreal experience, knowing that I could have killed us all. I remember saying to Bob, "Man, I almost killed us." To which he replied, "But we got lucky, and you didn't." I repeated it, and he just grabbed my shoulder and handed me the bottle of Jack Daniels. By the time we got back to Ohio, the Jack Daniels was gone.

From that point on, every time Rick's dad saw me, he asked "You keepin' the shiny side up these days?" That was his way of asking if I was keeping my vehicle right-side up.

It was a true recipe incident, with all of the ingredients present to make the cake: Terrible roads; unexpected black ice; an overconfident, young male driver; crashworthiness and handling near zero; and heavy, loose, dangerous objects. One more ingredient—such as a bottle flying in the wrong place or our vehicle encountering a guardrail, another car, a steep embankment, crossing over into oncoming traffic—and I wouldn't be writing this book.

What would have helped us in our situation? In other words, what ingredients could have been removed so that no figurative cake was made? For starters, our heavy, dangerous objects could have been securely stowed or placed in a trunk. We could have traveled in a vehicle with a lower center of gravity and better heat. We definitely should have been wearing our seat belts. The county in which the crash occurred could have implemented better road maintenance or warnings. Most of all, though, I needed to better understand the risks I faced as a driver and to adapt to the conditions appropriately.

Driving is definitely a case in which you don't want to have your cake and eat it, too. That is the purpose of this book: To help you increase your chances of surviving the drive, beginning with how to choose a safer vehicle, to using the available safety options in your vehicle, to understanding risky driver behaviors and how to avoid them.

Thanks for reading.

General Resources

http://www.census.gov/compendia/statab/2012/tables/12s1103.pdf

http://www.nhtsa.gov/FARS

http://www.cdc.gov/media/releases/2014/p1007-crash-injuries.html

http://www-nrd.nhtsa.dot.gov/Pubs/812006.pdf

https://www.fhwa.dot.gov/policyinformation/pubs/hf/pl11028/chapter4.cfm

http://www.distraction.gov/downloads/pdfs/driver-distraction-commercial-vehicle-operations.pdf

http://www.distraction.gov/downloads/pdfs/the-100-car-naturalistic-driving-study.pdf

How to *Survive the Drive* and Reduce Your Crash Risk

1   Chapter 1: Know Your Car and Your Options

Pick the right vehicle, or consider alternative transportation

10   Chapter 2: Low-hanging Fruit: Simple Ways to Reduce Your Risk

Wear seat belts, adjust your mirrors, reduce your speed, and be prepared

24   Chapter 3: Don't Hit Anything

Become an efficient and alert defensive driver

46   Chapter 4: Adapt, Overcome, and Survive

Adjust to the road conditions, the weather, the vehicle, and yourself

62   Chapter 5: Do Not Mix Mind-altering Substances with Driving

Know how testosterone, alcohol, and drugs affect crash risk

74   Chapter 6: Be Attentive and Alert

Keep your eyes on the road, and watch out for trucks

96   Chapter 7: Be Kind and Caring

Avoid being an aggressive driver and putting others in danger

104   Chapter 8: Be a Helicopter Parent…for This!

Find out the greatest risks facing teen drivers and how to train your teen to drive

126   Chapter 9: Senior Drivers: Rage Against the Dying of the Light

Understand older driver mobility and how to remain a safe driver for longer

134   Chapter 10: Motorcycles and a Few Tips for Motorcyclists

Become a safe, proficient rider and understand your unique risks

146   Chapter 11: The Crystal Ball: Be Ready for the Future

Find out what's in store for the future of vehicle design and safety

162   Final Thoughts: Question What You Read and Hear

Chapter 1.

Know Your Car and Your Options

Physics 101: F=MA

The very first lesson to remember while driving is that roadways are full of objects of unusual size and weight (mass) moving at high rates of speed (acceleration). This can create tremendous forces, particularly in a crash. If you took physics in high school, this is what your physics teacher tried to teach you:

Force = Mass x Acceleration, or F=MA.

What does this mean? Well, if you want to increase your chances of survival during a crash, slower speeds are better (although, as I will discuss later, too slow can also create force in a crash). Avoiding objects of increased mass will also reduce the potential for high forces and lessen the severity of crashes. The easiest lesson to learn here is to **STAY AWAY FROM TRUCKS**...unless, of course, you are a truck driver. We'll talk in more detail about this point later because I can't emphasize it enough.

A side note to the F=MA lesson is that it is always better to be on the high mass side versus the low mass side of any crash. Therefore, if you find yourself in a crash situation, you want to be the one primarily exerting most of the force as opposed to absorbing most of the force. Think of a head-on crash between a locomotive and a car traveling at equal speeds. While the train engineer will barely feel the impact, the car driver will, though for a short period of time for obvious reasons.

Based on this lesson, here are a couple of ideas to consider when choosing a vehicle.

What kind of car should I buy to reduce my risk?

1. Kill the planet and drive a big car if you have no other choice.

   I hesitate to say this, but all else being equal, the bigger the car, the more likely you are to survive a serious crash. Of course, there are a lot of practical trade-offs to this alternative, including increased cost for gas and a substantially negative environmental impact. Be that as it may, big cars generally help you survive a crash more effectively than small cars because they weigh more and typically sit up higher so that more of the forces are transmitted through the body of the car.

2. You better start swimming or you will sink like a stone, for the cars, they are a changin'.

   Having said the above about mass (that is, the bigger the better), the newer the car, the safer the car. And, in general, the more expensive the car model, the safer the car. If you find yourself saying "Wow, rich people have the capability to be safer than poor people," you are absolutely (unfortunately) right. However, there is good news. Unlike many aspects of income inequality, the gap regarding the ability to purchase a safe car has been narrowing for a number of years. In fact, low-cost, newer cars can be very safe. The key is to look at the government safety ratings, but be aware that the scales are different for different sized cars (MASS!). Therefore, I recommend that you put yourself and your family in the safest car that you can, given all of the trade-offs above.

Our friends at the Insurance Institute for Highway Safety (IIHS) conduct studies periodically that determine the number of fatal crashes per million vehicles of a particular model on the road. These studies include a variety of makes and models. Recent IIHS studies have found that new vehicles are improving greatly in crashworthiness and even crash avoidance technology, with fatality rates overall dropping with each model year. Based on the information above, you can guess which kinds of vehicles are generally the safest: Those that are bigger and heavier and new(er) vehicles with more safety features. Vehicles that sit up higher also factor into increased safety because most, if not all, of the force will be transmitted through the entire body in this type of vehicle, regardless of the height of what you may hit. What this all means is that SUVs dominate the list, with a minivan or two sprinkled in. At the bottom of the list are compacts and subcompacts, even those that received a five-star safety rating from IIHS.

This is all good information, and you should pay attention to it. However, you do need to be a little careful in how you interpret the results. For example, the "best" group of vehicles are generally not driven by younger drivers as much, they generally are not purchased by anyone who is a car enthusiast since they are bigger, and they are probably used more by families. Thus, they are driven by folks who don't tend to crash much. The Jalopnik website has a good discussion about the 10 best and 10 worst cars based on recent IIHS data. It should also be noted that the IIHS data are not corrected for miles driven. For example, if you drive a lot of miles, you may tend to drive a smaller, more fuel-efficient car.

Despite the limitations of the IIHS data, the underlying trends are undeniable. For example, nine of the vehicles listed under the 2011 model year category of the IIHS results had ZERO fatalities per million vehicles on the road. Even 10 years ago, there wasn't one vehicle on that list with a zero fatality rating per million vehicles.

However, buyer beware: Before you purchase one of these vehicles and start feeling invincible on the road, keep in mind that the crash fatality rate increased in the U.S. in 2012 for the first time in a number of years. In other words, we have a long way to go—likely decades—before fatalities occurring on the road may approach zero. Therefore, it's imperative to keep reading this book!

Physics 102: Safety Factors beyond Weight and My 1971 VW Bus

The modern car is an amazing feat of engineering. In addition to the obvious performance and luxury features, newer vehicles are designed to transmit the force of a crash around the passenger compartment and provide "landing surfaces" (airbags). Everything from collapsible steering columns to shatterproof glass to crumple zones, seat belt tensioners, and up to 11 airbags make the cars of today much, much safer than cars of even recent past. All of these factors minimize the damage to drivers and passengers. This ability to essentially protect the driver and/or passengers during a crash is known as the vehicle's crashworthiness.

By contrast, let's consider my 1971 VW Bus. (Remember, the '73 got totaled in the intro to this book.) While driving my bus, my feet were essentially inches away from the front bumper. My mid-section was mere inches from the steering wheel. The only redeeming fact in that regard was that the wheel made for a great place to hang on in a rollover crash. If you drove this bus and were concerned about crashworthiness, you mounted the spare tire on the front to provide more cushion in case of a frontal collision. There were no airbags, no door impact beams, and no heat to speak of. Horsepower in these vehicles was pretty non-existent, which is probably why many of us of a certain generation are still alive today.

Since my '71 VW, cars have come a long way and vary significantly. We've talked about size and weight changes, but there are also pretty big differences between makes and models of the same relative weight and the same year of manufacture. Do yourself and your family a favor and look at the National Highway Traffic Safety Administration (NHTSA) Star Rating or the ratings from the IIHS. There, you can find plenty of helpful information about the crashworthiness of almost any car—new or used—that you may want to buy.

I was fortunate enough to be able to buy my kids newer cars. Technically, I bought my kids half of the car and they bought the other half with money they saved or received over the years, primarily from their grandparents. I told them they could get any car they wanted, as long as it was a Honda Civic. There are plenty of good choices out there, and while the Civic doesn't have a lot of mass, it does consistently have high safety ratings from both NHTSA and IIHS. The Civic is also environmentally friendly, reliable, economical, holds its value, and is relatively inexpensive. It has a full complement of airbags, low horsepower (important!), and a feature I *really* like: The seat belt reminder never quits. In other words, the car pings a warning every mile forever and ever if you don't wear your seat belt. I essentially knew that my kids would always be belted.

My son, Chris, still has his 2007 Civic with more than 100,000 miles on it. However, like many teens, my daughter, Emily, no longer has her 2008 Civic. After my wife, Melissa, and I sent Emily away to college, we went on a month-long trip to Australia and New Zealand to give some lectures about distracted driving. While we were gone, Emily came home from college during Labor Day to see friends. On her way back to college, she was driving in a torrential rainstorm (1.5 inches per hour), hydroplaned at the bottom of a big hill, spun around at highway speeds, and hit the guardrail. Three airbags deployed; she hit her head on the front airbag and the side curtain airbag hard enough to break her glasses and suffer a concussion. I got a call in New Zealand at 4 a.m. that started with the words "Don't freak out."

What do you think would have happened had she not had a car with airbags? Or if she had been unbelted and out of her normal driving position when the airbags deployed? The potential was certainly there for permanent brain injury, or worse. Then I really would have freaked out.

Hydroplaning is tested at the VTTI-affiliated Global Center for Automotive Performance Simulation (GCAPS); still image from GCAPS video

Don't Expose Yourself, or Others

It is important to note that all of the odds you see in this book are not zero. Even when you have done everything you can to be safer or you experience a protective effect where your odds of being in a crash are less than 1.0, *you are still at some risk*. The only way to make your odds of being killed or injured in a crash while driving zero is not to drive! This is the concept of exposure. If you drive less, take public transit more, drive in better weather, and drive on safer roads, you reduce your risk by reducing your exposure. This will be an important concept throughout this book, and it is something that you should consider as you decide whether—and how—to get from Point A to Point B.

There are a few simple, alternative ways to reduce your exposure and the exposure of others without having to stay home all of the time:

1. Get out of the driver's seat, and save the planet while saving yourself. One way to manage your risk is to take more public transit and ride buses. A transit bus and a motorcoach are safer than a car. They have significant mass; are easy to see; and are operated by alert, sober, and attentive drivers in the majority of cases. It is a rare, although concerning, event when a driver of this type of heavy vehicle falls asleep at the wheel or is distracted to the point of causing a crash that inevitably involves many people. And, as the old transportation joke about public transportation goes, a bus is "a vehicle that takes you from where you aren't to where you don't want to go with people you don't want to ride with." So, I know that many of you can't or won't heed this advice. It's still an alternative to consider, though.

2. Put your kids on the school bus, go home, and have another cup of coffee. From a transportation perspective, there really are fewer places safer for your kids than a school bus. These buses have large mass; are very noticeable given that they are giant orange vehicles that feature flashing lights; and, like all buses and motorcoaches, are almost always operated by reasonably alert, trained, and sober drivers. Having said that, it is important to reinforce to your kids how to enter and exit a school bus, which is when almost all of the risks occur in this scenario.

General Resources

www.iihs.org

http://jalopnik.com/these-are-the-ten-cars-youre-most-likely-to-die-driving-1682672803

http://www-nrd.nhtsa.dot.gov/Pubs/811856.pdf

http://www.safercar.gov/Safety+Ratings

Chapter 2.

Low-hanging Fruit:
Simple Ways to Reduce Your Risk

Seat Belts: You May Not Get Caught, but Wear Them Anyway

Crashes can be exceptionally violent events with tremendous accelerations and forces applied in virtually any direction. However, the good news is that you have seat belts. This can't be stressed enough: There is no better option you have to protect yourself in a crash than to wear a seat belt. We have all heard it for years, but it's a fact:

You *double your odds* (odds = 2.0) of an injury or fatality in a crash if you aren't wearing a seat belt.

For a head-on crash, of which there are approximately 10,000 each year, you are *five times more likely* to walk away without a serious injury or dying if you have an airbag AND are wearing a seat belt.

Essentially, your odds are 0.2 if you are involved in a head-on crash but have an airbag AND wear your seat belt. That's a tremendous protective effect. However, the AND part is important. Airbags can actually cause injuries in crashes when the driver is unbelted and out of the normal driving position. And, let's face it, airbags aren't going to be of much help if a driver is unbelted and is ejected out of his or her vehicle during a rollover crash.

The good news is that most of us wear seat belts, and the numbers of those wearing seat belts are increasing every year. The national seat belt use rate is about 87%. Oregon wins the driving safety award for the highest seat belt usage within the U.S., with a rate of 98.2%. South Dakota has the lowest rate with 68.7%. Interestingly, the one state that has no seat belt law is New Hampshire (think live free and die…whoops, I meant live free OR die), but at 73%, it still has a higher seat belt use rate than South Dakota.

In big, round numbers, the seat belt usage rate is about 5% lower for males (testosterone allows them to fend off airbags with a single karate chop), 10% lower for rural states (which is ironic since roll-over crashes are more common in such locations), and 10% lower for states with secondary seat belt laws (that is, you can't get pulled over just because you are not wearing your seat belt) or no seat belt law at all (New Hampshire).

Another good reason to wear a seat belt was demonstrated by my friend, Rick. I was driving my '71 VW Bus one evening on the way to buy beer. Rick was sitting sideways in the passenger seat, leaning against his door. As I made a sweeping left-hand turn through the near-empty parking lot, the passenger-side door popped open, and Rick flew out, did a backwards roll, and landed on his feet. Luckily, he only ended up with a few minor bruises. He had a glass bottle in his hand that broke during the roll, and what was left of the bottle was still in his hand.

Here is some cheap, but effective, advice regarding seat belt use: If you are a lawmaker, pass a primary seat belt law for both front and rear seat occupants if your state doesn't have such a law. You will save a lot of lives and be a hero, honest. If you are a police officer or supervisor of police officers, enforcement of whatever laws are on the books helps significantly. I know it is a hard law to enforce, but there are ways to do it. Oregon or Washington may be good places to look for ideas since they have higher compliance rates.

If you are a driver, husband, wife, parent, or child, make sure every-one wears their seat belts for even the shortest trip. You will likely get into a couple of crashes in your lifetime, and seat belts really, re-ally, really could save your life. Seat belts also keep you from getting into an unintentional wrestling match with everyone else in your car during a crash. While his weight may not seem important while tak-ing a leisurely stroll or going to the movies, having your 200-pound husband flying at you out of control in a car during a crash can cause serious injury. So, either make him wear his seat belt or put him on a serious diet.

Speaking of unbelted mammals of large size traveling in a car…

Saving "man's best friend"
and your toolbox while saving yourself

I was riding along with my friend, Mark, one day on our way to a skiing trip in Colorado. The road was icy and my brakes were not working so well (pretty spongy) in my old '66 Baja Beetle. However, being undaunted and 20 years old, we pressed ahead through the snow in search of slopes. Our skis were bungee-corded relatively securely to a roof rack on top. My Malamute, Wolf, was riding along with us in the back seat. Wolf was a BIG DOG.

As we were traveling along, the car in front of us stopped suddenly, and we slammed into it. Even with no shoulder belt (that particular car model only had lap belts), I would have been able to keep my face from hitting the steering wheel except for—you guessed it—Wolf slamming into the back of my seat. The driver seat had no seatback lock lever or head rest, which meant I slammed my face into the steering wheel anyway. If that wasn't bad enough, Wolf came over the top of the seat and landed on top of me, creating (luckily) only a few bruises and cuts. He also popped out the front windshield, which made for a very cold ride home. To add insult to (literally) injury, Wolf, although relatively unscathed, was very scared and proceeded to pee all over Mark and me while he struggled to find his footing. Since the Baja had a fiberglass front and was lightweight, the impact itself caused little damage to the car in front of us. However, our roof rack broke loose and slid up and over the car in front, peeling paint off that car from the trunk to the hood.

The moral of the story is this: Think of your pets, and anything else heavy in your car, as a potential projectile heading straight for you—or rolling around with you—in a crash. There are a variety of products available to belt your dog in the back seat, or dividers that separate you from your pet. It's better for them, and it's better for you, to use such products.

And keep your gold bars or dumbbells (or sledge hammers, chainsaws, and toolboxes) in the trunk!

Tom and Wolf; from the author's personal photo collection

Physics 103: Momentum, Acceleration, Deceleration, and Speed

Speed(ing) kills

If you ask anyone who has been studying driving safety for a long time what factors are most involved in fatal crashes, they will tell you belts, booze, and speed, although driver distraction has been recently added to this discussion. Some facts to consider:

In general, speeding more than 10 mph over the speed limit or too fast for conditions increases your odds of being in a crash by *about 12 times* **(odds = 12.0).**

It's really easy to speed in a modern car. Even economy vehicles can go very fast; much faster than is safe or legal. I will talk at some length about alcohol and other types of impairment later in this book, but it should be emphasized upfront that alcohol impacts both your driving performance and your driving behavior. When it comes to alcohol, drivers' judgment can also suffer a blow, leading to traveling at high speeds and not wearing seat belts. Consider this:

If you are drunk at the legal blood alcohol content limit (BAC = 0.08%), you are *2.5 times more likely* (odds = 2.5) to die while speeding than if you are sober.

There are numerous reasons why your crash risk increases due to speeding. These reasons include a greater chance of losing control of the vehicle, creating greater speed differences between you and cars traveling the speed limit, having less time to react to a hazard, and having less usable sight distances because you have less time to react. Speed also increases the probability that you will be injured or killed in a crash. This is really just a matter of F=MA. In this case, forces increase significantly with speed (that is, acceleration). At some point, the forces can overwhelm even the most crashworthy of cars. Crash types also change with speeding, including an increase in road departure crashes that lead to rollovers and collisions with fixed objects, such as oak trees.

As with almost all risk-related contributing factors, *males are more likely than females* to be involved in a speeding-related fatal crash. (In Chapter 5, I talk more about testosterone as it relates to driving.) Younger drivers speed more than older drivers, with the speeding-related crash rate *almost twice as high* for drivers under the age of 34.

Extreme speeding is certainly one of the most dangerous behaviors a driver can undertake. The risk here increases exponentially because of all the factors described above *plus* the increased potential to experience a severe impact with either a moving or fixed object. Take the following scenario, for example:

If you are speeding more than 30 mph over the speed limit, your odds of being injured in a crash are between *30 and 50 times higher* (odds = 30.0 – 50.0) than if you are traveling within 10 mph of the speed limit.

In terms of speed selection, you want to be traveling close to the speed limit and/or the speed of traffic around you. If you are slightly over the speed limit, chances are you will be in sync with traffic for the most part and will have to pass and get passed the least, meaning you can avoid more possible conflicts.

One thing I learned a long time ago is this: There are numerous times you don't want to be number one. This is true at a party where it's better to be the guy or gal who has had the second or third most to drink rather than the guy or gal who has had the most to drink. These "number ones" are often the talk of the party, though not necessarily in a good way, and they are often in trouble with their significant others. The same analogy applies to speed selection. Pay enough attention to make sure you are not the fastest driver around. If you are the fastest, you are not only at the highest risk of a serious crash, you are also likely to get a ticket sooner or later.

The moral of the story is to go with the flow!

Speed (differential) also kills

Your primary goal as a driver is to avoid conflicts with other vehicles. If you don't have any conflicts—meaning, you don't occupy the same space at the same time as other vehicles—you will never hit anyone else. The probability of a conflict increases under a variety of circumstances, including at intersections when your path literally crosses those of other drivers, while changing lanes, and when there is a speed differential. As mentioned previously, both your crash risk and the resulting severity of the crash increase substantially when you speed. However, there is also greater risk of a crash if you travel significantly slower than other drivers. During both instances, you are creating what we call the speed differential, which results in a greater chance of a severe crash.

Think of your crash risk due to speed differentials as a U-shaped curve: The peaks of that curve—or your significant increased risk of an injury or fatality—represent the speed differential created by either driving much too fast or much too slow. Essentially, you do not want to deviate more than 10 mph from the speed at which the rest of traffic is traveling, or your risk will increase...a lot.

This brings up an important point: If you can't maintain a reasonable speed for any reason—say, you lost the number three cylinder in your VW bus or you ran out of gas—get the car off of the road. If you can't get the car off of the road, get out of the car, get safely onto the shoulder, run in the direction from which you were traveling in your vehicle (while well onto the shoulder!), and wave your arms to warn other drivers. Really. You will look much less foolish than if someone hits your car at a speed differential of 60 mph.

A few winters ago, I was traveling with my friend and colleague, Andy Petersen, on a mission to get my truck unstuck. (Andy and his group design and build all of our data collection systems used in the VTTI naturalistic driving studies. A version of those systems is shown on the next page. You can read more about the systems and our studies at www.vtti.vt.edu.) As I was following Andy, we came upon a curved bridge where we saw a car lying on its side in the right lane. A woman was in this car, sticking her head up through the driver's side window, waving for help. Turns out that the bridge had iced over before the rest of the road, and she spun out and somehow hit the guardrail and rolled over. What should I do? It was a terrible situation because traffic was still moving fast, sight distance was limited due to the curve, and the bridge was slick. The chances were very high that someone could hit her at a high rate of speed, and she was certainly in no position to be protected from such a crash.

So, having limited options in a generally unsafe situation, I backed my truck down the shoulder to a straight stretch with good sight distance and traction. I parked half of my truck in the right lane and half on the shoulder. Again, this wasn't the safest option, but I thought it would work to get other drivers to both slow down and change lanes. I turned on my hazards and put out a triangle reflector. Then, I got out of the truck and went to help Andy get the woman out of her car and safely off of the roadway. Luckily, and despite the fact that I had created a hazard myself, cars slowed, and traffic eventually backed up before encountering the crashed vehicle. The point here is this: There is no way I would have stayed in my truck and done nothing, because getting that woman out of the car was of paramount importance due to the speed differential she was facing and the fact that the crash site could have caused an unexpected event for other drivers. I also would have been at risk by staying in my stopped truck.

A VTTI-developed data collection system dubbed the MiniDAS; photo courtesy of VTTI

Eliminate Blind Spots

Many cars these days are designed such that you can effectively eliminate virtually all blind spots *if* you adjust your mirrors appropriately. There are several important points to consider when adjusting your mirrors:

1. You don't need to see the side of your car.

   Many people adjust their side view mirrors so that a lot of their car is in the view. What you want to do instead is adjust your mirrors out to the point where you can *just barely* see the side of your car.

2. You need to use whatever is there.

   In my family, two of our cars have the small, round convex mirrors attached to the main mirror to help eliminate blind spots. These supplementary mirrors help, but it takes a little effort and practice to make sure you are using them and not just looking at the main mirror. There are other types of mirrors, including some European models that feature a regular mirror towards the inside and a convex mirror towards the outside. The same rules apply, though: Focus on using what is there.

3. Checking your blind spot is still a good idea.

   I have convinced myself that my car has no blind spot, but I check it anyway. Why, you ask? Because I don't completely trust that there isn't a blind spot for every kind of motorcycle, scooter, or small car on the road. And, hey, there is nothing wrong with double-checking!

4. Make sure the mirrors aren't creating blind spots!

   I have seen cases in which the mirrors themselves create blind spots to the left and right. This is particularly true of, say, a large truck or van with very tall mirrors. Sometimes, the combination of the mirror and the vehicle pillar can hide bicycles, pedestrians, and even scooters or motorcycles. If you drive such a vehicle, it may be important to lean forward at intersections or to check three times to make sure nothing is hiding.

Be Prepared for the Snowpocalypse, Snowmageddon, or Any Other Next Great Catastrophe . . . It Could Happen to You!

I used to live in the mountains of Colorado with my first wife, Joellen (we got married when we were 19, which turned out to be too young). I was commuting up and down Highway 285, which was often a fascinating drive that fluctuated between 5,280 feet and 9,000 feet in elevation. One Friday night, Joellen and I went with some friends to a laser light show in Denver (Google it, kids). We were heading up the massive Highway 285 hill in a rainstorm in my '71 VW bus. As often happened as we increased in elevation, the rain turned to freezing rain, and the highway became a sheet of ice. However, being a daily commuter up this road and being well-seasoned following the rollover in my '73 VW bus, I was prepared for these conditions.

We had chains, sleeping bags, a catalytic heater stashed in a storage area under a seat (because we had learned to securely stow all heavy, loose objects), pack boots, down coats, etc. The scene was surrealistic as we continued our trek; there were many non-experienced commuters heading into the mountains for the weekend. As a result, cars were stuck everywhere in both lanes and on both shoulders. No one was going anywhere because there was a Jersey barrier, which is a continuous concrete barrier often seen on highways. It all meant there was no way for plows or salt trucks to get through the scene. So, with nothing better to do, we cruised around on foot for a bit to survey the damage and assist as needed.

Soon, I encountered an ill-prepared, frantic woman in a mink stole and high heels who asked for my help. I know she was frantic because, in a thick foreign accent, she said "Help me, I'm frantic!" I explained to her that she may as well relax for a while because she had plenty of gas to run the heat in her Thunderbird and a new enough car that she wouldn't experience fume problems.

A few cars ahead, I helped a local sheriff put on his chains because he had no gloves. As I continued to walk, I heard a car ahead really gunning the engine. As I got closer, I could tell that the male driver had put chains on his tires and had apparently forged a path forward. He was, therefore, trying to get out, and with great enthusiasm.

Unfortunately, the road was icy enough to the point that he was just spinning in place. Remember this guy's tire chains? Well, at some point during this spectacle, part of a chain came loose and ruptured the gas tank. Sparks from the spinning chains ignited the gas, tank, and, inevitably, the whole car. Fortunately, the driver and his passenger escaped, but the car was engulfed in flames 15 or 20 feet high. There was nothing anyone could do other than watch in amazement. Joellen and I sat there on the Jersey barrier and watched for about an hour until the car had basically burned itself out. At that point, the local fire department managed to close the downhill side of the highway and get a pumper truck down the icy hill to deal with the fire. The fire department then proceeded to pump hundreds of gallons of water on the fire to make sure it was completely out. Of course, the water they pumped out only turned to more ice. Nearly six hours later, the road was opened again, and we made it the rest of the way home.

The moral of the story here is to carry what you might need should the unexpected happen: Chains (where needed), flares, flashlights, reflective triangles, etc. Have a good spare tire and basic tools, because even these days you may have limited cell coverage during a trip. You can buy cool little kits at any auto parts store at a minimal cost. I have friends who also stash some cash—a few hundred dollars will usually do—in their cars when taking a trip, just in case. It's much better to have it and not need it than to need it and not have it!

The other side of this "expect the unexpected" story comes by way of my friend and colleague, Zac Doerzaph. During one relatively Indian summer-like day in late November, Zac flew to Detroit from our home in Southwest Virginia on a business trip. He had a light jacket and a normal suitcase full of business-casual clothes appropriate for the weather. A few days later, Zac headed back home, making the return trip in a car since he was taking a last-minute opportunity to shuttle back one of our test vehicles.

Well, Zac ran into an unexpected blizzard that dumped about 18 inches of snow within a few hours, crippling the West Virginia turnpike on which he was traveling. The vehicle he was driving was not made for heavy snow, and he lacked any emergency supplies. The car wasn't his, and he had not expected to drive back home, much less spend the next 12 hours with numerous stranded motorists while authorities—including the National Guard—worked diligently to open the roadway one vehicle at a time. He had nothing with him, except slacks and polo shirts. He had no cell phone charger, very bad reception, limited food since he gave most of what he had to a nearby mother for her toddler, and he was nearly out of gas. To deal with plummeting temperatures and to do his best to stay warm throughout the night, Zac put on both pairs of pants he had, made a turban out of his polo shirts, and curled into a ball on the floorboards and away from the cold glass of the vehicle. He got invited into the cab of a semi to warm up, but declined the kind offer…at least, he figured, until he was desperate. Zac spent a very uncomfortable eight-hour night trying to stay warm and carefully conserve what little gas remained in the tank in the hopes that a plow may clear the way.

The point is simple: It's better to be prepared.

Colorado driving; from the author's personal photo collection

General Resources

http://www.cdc.gov/Motorvehiclesafety/seatbelts/facts.html

http://aje.oxfordjournals.org/content/153/3/219.full

http://www-nrd.nhtsa.dot.gov/pubs/806572.pdf

http://www-nrd.nhtsa.dot.gov/Pubs/811875.pdf

http://www-nrd.nhtsa.dot.gov/Pubs/812030.pdf

http://www-nrd.nhtsa.dot.gov/Pubs/812080.pdf

http://www-nrd.nhtsa.dot.gov/Pubs/812021.pdf

Chapter 3.

Don't Hit Anything

Defensive Driving 101:
Don't Invade My Space

The goal of defensive driving is to get you to your destination in a safe manner, having successfully anticipated hazards and avoided conflicts with other vehicles or objects on the road. When it comes to driving, the best defense is not a good offense, even though there may be times when most of us wish for offensive weapons in our cars. Nothing fancy, just a few James Bond/Aston Martin kinds of machine guns and smoke bombs. The funny thing is, if you mention that to the hardware guys at VTTI, they actually start to figure out how to do it…Anyway, I digress. The point is, don't confuse defensive driving with driving aggressively. The National Highway Traffic Safety Administration (NHTSA) defines aggressive driving as "occurring when 'an individual commits a combination of moving traffic offenses so as to endanger other persons or property.'" Basically, driving aggressively means you're driving like a bat out of hell with no regard to the well-being of others. I'll talk more about aggressive driving in Chapter 7.

Below are some tips to move you *safely* from Point A to Point B as a defensive driver while ensuring you do not compromise the safety of your fellow transportation users. Along the way, I'll give you points on how to avoid being the aggressor.

It's all about time and space

As you hurtle through space in your shiny metal box of unusual size and weight, it is important to stay away from all of the other shiny boxes of unusual sizes and weights. The best way to do this is to increase the space, *and the time*, between you and everything else that you can. I emphasize time because it is sometimes more important than space. For example, if you were 60 feet away from a car in a parking lot while traveling 10 mph, it would take more than four seconds until you hit the car. That's relatively an eternity in terms of having enough time to avoid a crash. By contrast, you would only have a little more than 0.5 seconds to avoid a crash under the same distance while traveling 70 mph on an interstate.

Of course, an easy way to increase time and space is to NOT TAIL-GATE. Following too closely decreases your space and time, obviously. There are many, many crash cases each year that begin with this ingredient present to make our figurative cake: Following too closely. In the grand scheme of things, not tailgating means you will get to where you're going two seconds later. Other ways to create more space include moving to the left lane to pass a disabled vehicle on the shoulder of a highway and giving bicycles, pedestrians, and parked cars a wide berth as you pass. These probably seem obvious, but if you think about them in terms of giving yourself more space and time to react if something unexpected occurs, it becomes a good defensive driving habit.

A most important defense: Do not interact with heavy vehicles

Here is another friendly physics lesson: A long-haul truck is 40 tons of unforgiving steel hurtling the length of a football field every three seconds. In other words—as you will read time and time again throughout this book—STAY AWAY FROM TRUCKS.

photo courtesy of VTTI

The vast majority of truck drivers are professional, safe drivers. But, just like all other types of drivers, "most" does not mean "all," and even good truck drivers occasionally get in bad situations.

About 10 years ago, there was a multi-truck collision on an interstate near my home. The crash originated when a truck mowed into a line of stopped traffic while traveling at about 65 mph, with no indication of the truck driver braking beforehand. The truck driver was likely drowsy or distracted, resulting in a deadly recipe. The situation subsequently created a hazard for other drivers. Crashes like this are not terribly frequent, but they are always terrible. In this case, emergency workers arrived on the scene and worked for several hours to separate two Class 8 (semi) trucks. After working for about two hours or so, they realized for the first time that there was a minivan sandwiched between the two trucks. The minivan was about one-third of its original length; all four of its occupants were killed instantly in the crash. There is no airbag, no crumple zone, no five-star vehicle of any weight that would have allowed that family to survive. The forces generated in such a crash were just too great.

With that in mind, here are some facts about trucks from my friend, former student, and colleague, Rich Hanowski, and his staff in the VTTI Center for Truck and Bus Safety:

1. 10% of truck drivers account for 40% to 50% of crash and near-crash risks. Your only problem: You don't know which ones are part of the 10%.

2. One out of every 25 trucks you see on the road has a driver falling asleep at the wheel.

3. Even when truck drivers are awake and alert, they are doing some kind of secondary task (like talking on a cell phone, reading something, etc.) more than 25% of the time.

4. A texting truck driver has *23 times* the risk of being involved in a safety-critical event compared to a driver just traveling down the road. And truckers *do* text!

The moral of the story is that you should keep as much space and time between you and heavy trucks as possible. Doing so will really help your odds of avoiding a crash with a heavy truck, not only because truck drivers make mistakes, but because:

Two out of every three crashes **involving a car and a truck is the fault of the car driver.**

The large truck fatality rate per 100 million vehicle miles traveled is 1.42, while the fatality rate for cars is 1.31 per 100 million vehicle miles traveled. So many of us can do better around truck drivers. The following tips may be of help when steering clear of trucks:

1. If you are following a truck, stay back until you are ready to pass.

2. If there is a vehicle ahead of you passing a truck, wait until after that vehicle completes the pass before starting your pass. Don't ride along beside the truck.

3. When you are passing on either side of a truck, be wary of its blind spots. Those danger zones differ from cars and are located anywhere behind the truck and alongside the cab, particularly just in front of the cab on the right. Our friends at the Federal Motor Carrier Safety Administration (FMCSA) have good information about the "No Zone" of a truck. Some truck carriers also display a placard on the back of trucks indicating blind spots. The bottom line is to stay away from these areas while you drive!

4. Always pass trucks briskly, even if you have to speed a little to pass safely. When you do make your pass, do so quickly. You do not want to linger in the blind spots of a truck for any length of

time. Just keep a copy of this book in your vehicle and show it to the cop if you get pulled over for speeding up to pass a truck; tell 'em a safety professional told you to do it.

5. Trucks can't stop as fast as you can, so don't cut them off. Don't pass and then slow down; give truck drivers plenty of room on your briskly executed lane change.

Expect the unexpected

Periodically, I get asked to serve as an expert witness in legal cases involving a crash. At least once per year, I get a call from an attorney representing a client—on either side of the case—involved in a crash where a car or truck slammed into a line of vehicles with no signs of braking or slowing. Usually, the defendant was driving on the interstate and hit a plaintiff in a stalled car/truck/hay wagon/etc. More often than not, the crash occurred during ideal driving conditions: Dry, clear, during the day, with a long sight distance. These crashes left behind no, or very short, skid marks before the vehicles hit.

You may ask "How could this be? How can you miss a stopped vehicle in broad daylight?" That's typically what the courts ask as well. The driver must have been looking down at something, or must have been falling asleep at the wheel, right? The answer is: Yes…most of the time the driver was looking somewhere else, even if it was just a random glance away from the roadway. However, regardless of whether the offending driver was distracted or fatigued, the stopped vehicle in the majority of these scenarios violated the expectations of the driver. Essentially, the stopped vehicle created a key ingredient to make our figurative cake, thus resulting in a crash. No one *expects* a vehicle to be stopped in the left lane of an interstate, at least on a rural interstate. It is a very rare event. And humans are notoriously bad at being alert and ready to respond to a rare event, a fact I will discuss at length in the last chapter of this book.

I have two words of advice here:

1. Practice trying to anticipate where hazards may be lurking.

    It could be a service van blocking the sight distance to an inter-section, or a "work zone ahead" or "mowing" sign on the inter-state that may create unstable traffic and a sudden slowdown. The blue lights of a police car almost always make someone hit the brakes to avoid a ticket, even if traffic is flowing only slightly above the speed limit. The hazard could be an oncoming car that is fully or partially blocked from your vision by cars in the turn lane opposite to you. You may encounter a crowded street full of pedestrians in a college town after a football game.

    There are just too many cases to name. The point is to work on being alert and wary when the situation demands it. Focus your attention where something may happen quickly, which is usually the closest threat. Don't make assumptions about what you can't see and what other road users might do.

2. Stay engaged in the driving task so that you can brake hard and fast at any moment if needed.

    This is a hard piece of advice to follow, and I will talk about this point throughout the book. In general, though, **KEEP YOUR EYES ON THE ROAD**. Be aware that you have a primary task (driving) to which you must pay attention by scanning the environment, controlling your vehicle, and being ready to avoid hazards.

Don't violate the expectations of other drivers

The flip side to expecting the unexpected is to avoid being the cause of the unexpected. You will read this several times throughout the book, but you don't want other drivers to hit YOU because you vio-lated their expectations. That is, *you* do not want to be the key ingredient that results in the figurative cake being made. Some recurring themes are present in this scenario: Go the speed other drivers pretty much expect. Get your car off of the road if you have to stop. If you can't get your car off of the road, get out of the car, get to a safe place, and warn other drivers. When parking on the side of the street, check your mirrors before opening your car door. And, of course, follow the rules of the road, because that's what people expect.

My friend and colleague, John Lee, was having a beer with me recently. I was telling him about this book. In addition to a lot of good publishing advice, John shared one of his stories that illustrates a point about violating the expectations of other drivers. When John first began to drive, he missed an exit on the highway. Being quite young and inexperienced, it seemed like a good idea to back his car up on the interstate and then take the exit. No other cars were around when he started this process, but soon there was a car approaching (road scenarios can change quickly when cars are essentially traveling the length of a football field every three seconds). The car hit John from behind but was able to brake to the point where no one was hurt and there was relatively minor damage.

John, of course, thought that he was in serious trouble, would lose his newly received license for reckless driving, etc. A police officer arrived on the scene, got both licenses, and proceeded to interview the other driver. The officer then came to John's car and said, "Here is the police report so you can make an insurance claim. That guy had some crazy story about you backing up on the interstate…but I didn't believe him and gave him a ticket. You are free to go." John learned an important lesson that day about violating the expectations of other drivers, not to mention a lesson learned about luck!

When you run out of time and space, what is the best way to crash?

One of my favorite musicians is an artist named Todd Snider. (Todd, you may remember me, I am the guy with the gray beard singing out of key in the front row.) Todd wrote a very touching number called "45 miles" that is a story about the brief moment of time between realizing you are going to wreck your car and wrecking your car. As he sings in the preamble to the song, it only has one chord because he was "pressed for time."

Many of us have experienced exactly what Todd is talking about. On rare occasions (made rarer still if you continue reading this book), a situation is simply not salvageable and you are going to hit *something*.

It is first helpful to understand what drivers often do in this situation so that you can perhaps react well in what is a very short time period. I performed a study with my friend, colleague, and former student, Jon Hankey, in which we looked at driver behavior during imminent crash circumstances. The study was performed with several of our colleagues from the National Highway Traffic Safety Administration (NHTSA). This was Jon's dissertation when we were at the University of Iowa. Jon used a high-fidelity driving simulator for this study, creating scenarios in which drivers had to react to different cases where a vehicle pulled out in front of them at an intersection.

A very interesting result from this study was that, when drivers had the least amount of time to react and were faced with the most severe crash, *they reacted the slowest*. They were also just as likely to steer as they were to brake in such a circumstance. Why would this be, you ask? We believe it was because the drivers had no obvious option to avoid the crash in the brief moment/space they had to decide what to do. Since there wasn't an obvious ideal choice, it took these drivers longer to consider their options. This is probably also why roughly half of them began to brake first, while half of them steered first.

Another, probably less surprising, fact was that drivers steered their vehicles away from the direction in which the other vehicle was entering the roadway. For example, if the other vehicle was coming from the right, the drivers tended to steer left into the opposing lane of traffic. As I will discuss later, braking like hell and avoiding head-on collisions are really better strategies in virtually all circumstances like this.

Here's another example to illustrate what drivers often do when they are faced with the inevitable. I helped perform a study in the mid-1990s led by my friend, colleague, and former student, Mike Mollenhauer, which looked at driver emergency response on icy roads. This was a very cool study, literally and figuratively. We took drivers to the spillway of a dam in Iowa during January after having the local fire department come out and spray the area with water. We told the volunteer drivers that we were trying to determine how they liked a new kind of car on slick roads (deception, which is sometimes carefully done in our line of work, but not lying). After they drove around for a while on a course we laid out, we then slid a large object that looked very heavy and ominous (it wasn't) into their path, giving them little time to react. Of course, we made sure that the drivers were in no danger, but they didn't really know what it was they were going to hit and what damage might be done to the car.

The reason we did this study was that an interesting phenomenon had just occurred in history: Anti-lock brake systems, or ABS, had recently been introduced. While rear-end crashes decreased slightly with the advent of ABS, road departure crashes increased slightly despite all expectations to the contrary.

Before the creation of ABS, drivers would often try to steer but would still hit the car or object in the road because the vehicle was still skidding or sliding after the driver slammed on the brakes. Steering in a crash scenario without ABS more or less just gave the driver a false sense of security that he or she had some ounce of control. With ABS, however, drivers now had full steering control. If they steered to the right, lo and behold, they often went off the road.

The issue here was that, if you left the roadway, instead of hitting the car or object in front of you, you were more likely to be injured or killed because of a rollover or a collision with a fixed object, such as an oak tree.

We discovered two important points in this study. First, drivers usually steer to the right to avoid an object in front of them after slamming on the brakes. This occurs when drivers realize they don't have enough time and space to stop. As mentioned, steering to the right with ABS usually resulted in drivers going off the road.

The second important finding of this study was that most folks back then didn't know how to use ABS, despite the best efforts of car dealers everywhere. At the very least, the drivers in this particular study reverted back to the automatic behavior of "pumping the brakes" on ice, a maneuver we were all taught in the dark ages. However, you should "squeeze" the brakes hard until they chatter when driving a vehicle equipped with ABS. If you have never experienced the chatter, it can be a bit disconcerting, but it is a very good sign. The chatter should reassure you that your car is pumping the brakes for you at a much faster rate and more effectively than you can move your foot. Essentially, a modern car and a driver who knows how the car works make a great pair when it comes to avoiding crashes.

There are several other considerations that should guide our brief thoughts when faced with an imminent crash: Fixed objects, delta V, and vulnerable road users.

My friend, Gene Farber, who passed away a number of years ago and is mentioned in more detail later in this book, used to tell a story about his days working at Ford. Gene had the opportunity to actually sit in a car during a low-speed crash test. The test was essentially designed to run a car into a solid wall at 10 mph. Gene thought what most of us would think: "How bad could that be, it's only 10 mph?" It ended up being a shocking and bone-jarring experience for Gene, and he was physically sore for several days. Now, imagine what hitting an oak tree at 60 mph would feel like.

In terms of hitting a solid fixed object, a rule of thumb is that the potential for injury is the same as hitting a moving object at twice the speed. Cars are considered "moving" objects even when they are stopped because they move and deform (bend, crumple, etc.) when you hit them. This rule breaks down to some extent for head-on collisions because the moving object is about to exert tremendous force on you as part of the equation. This brings us to delta V, which is also known as change in velocity, or the total speed between two colliding objects. If you are traveling at, say, 60 mph, a head-on collision has a delta V of 120 mph when assuming the other car is also traveling at 60 mph. If you hit a stationary car while traveling at 60 mph, the delta V is just your speed.

Now I want to talk about vulnerable road users relative to crash risk. There are entire chapters of this book dedicated to the topic of vulnerable road users. These are typically pedestrians, cyclists, folks on scooters or mopeds, or motorcyclists. If there is any way to avoid hitting a vulnerable road user, you should do so. If you think back to the F=MA equation, you are on the side with a higher mass, meaning you are going to exert a whole lot of force with your vehicle. On top of that, these folks have very little protection against hurtling metal traveling at high rates of speed, so the outcome is often fatal for them. Killing someone, regardless of the circumstances, will change your life in a bad way on so many levels, not to mention the devastation you'll cause for everyone involved. Be alert, attentive, and courteous around vulnerable road users. Even if you have to wait 20 seconds to safely pass a bicyclist, their life is worth more than your time.

The reason I am telling you all of this is to give you a strategy for what to hit if you have limited choices and you know you are going to crash. I have seen alert, attentive, and sober drivers do some amazing things to avoid crashes, a fact discussed in greater detail in the last chapter of this book. However, if you are "pressed for time" in a crash scenario and can't really carefully consider your options, here are a few very simple rules that may help you:

1. Don't steer left, risking a head-on collision. Due to its significant delta V, a head-on collision has the highest injury and fatality rates of any crash type:

    Roughly three times higher* than a road departure crash and *41 times higher* than a rear-end crash.

    This is why you may have heard the phrase "take the ditch" in the context of dealing with someone crossing the center line heading towards you. But life is more complicated than that, and there are always exceptions. For instance, if you are in the left lane of a divided highway and have the choice between slamming into a line of stopped traffic at 60 mph (maybe because you were tired or distracted, or you were just not expecting stopped traffic) or steering left into the median, the median may be a good choice.

2. Don't take the ditch if you can help it. Although better than a head-on crash, road departure crashes are also very bad:

    Roughly 14 times higher* in terms of fatality and injury rates than a rear-end crash.

    Steering into a ditch may put you in the path of fixed objects, or could lead to a rollover. As described earlier, you may have a natural tendency to steer right. If so, try to keep your vehicle on the shoulder, if there is one and you can perform such a maneuver.

3. Brake like hell!

    A fascinating phenomenon about driver behavior is that most

drivers brake at only about 60% of the vehicle's braking ability before a rear-end crash. Braking to a car's limit is something we rarely do. Most often, we are worried about upsetting passengers or spilling coffee. Take the family out to the local shopping mall with no one around and *slam on the damn brakes*! Have everyone try it a few times. That way, you will be ready when you are about to crash and can hit the brakes hard and fast, with absolutely no hesitation. Believe me when I tell you that it's easier to apologize to your wife afterwards, and getting coffee stains out of your carpet at an auto detailer is cheaper than any trip to a body shop.

Again, there are some exceptions. If you brake to the limit of your car's ability, you should pat yourself on the back for that brief moment…until the driver behind you hits you because he or she is only braking at 60% capacity. Remember, if someone is behind you when you brake hard to avoid a crash, you're becoming the unexpected and violating expectations in such a scenario. But hey, at least you won't get a ticket, and your insurance rates won't go up.

Two words of advice here: Keep an extra copy of this book in your car to give to the person that just hit you so they will know to brake harder, and be alert and attentive so you can generally avoid having to brake hard and get hit from behind.

4. Buy a car that brakes like hell!

Our friends at NHTSA recently came out with an interesting statistic. Data released by the agency indicate that:

60% of fatal crashes are caused by inattentive drivers, based on 2013 information.

Those of us at VTTI have actually believed that for some time this key "cake" ingredient has been present in large quantities of crashes based on our study trends. However, the NHTSA report marks the first time such data have been substantiated in fatal crash information. Therefore, NHTSA is adding to its star rating system both crash imminent braking (meaning, the car brakes automatically if it believes you are about to crash) and dynamic braking (that is, the car senses that you hit the brakes hard and automatically takes you from the 60% capacity level to the maximum braking level the car can perform). This may help greatly with the fatal crash problem, but only time will tell since NHTSA decided not to require such features on all cars, though it can choose to mandate such.

Hit Bambi, Thumper, and Rocky if you have to… but maybe not Bullwinkle

Pop quiz: What's the most dangerous animal in the United States?
   a)   All venomous snakes
   b)   All sharks
   c)   Black widow and brown recluse spiders
   d)   Deer

The answer is deer, by a large margin. State Farm estimates that, each year, more than one million crashes and 150 fatalities in the U.S. are caused by the presence of deer. By contrast, about six people die in the U.S. from wild venomous snake bites per year (which does not include another six or so who die from "snake handling" or religious ceremonies); about seven die from spider bites. At most, shark attacks cause one fatality every two years in the United States.

Senator John Warner (Virginia, now retired) helped VTTI become the National Surface Transportation Safety Center for Excellence, which was a congressional designation. When the building housing the center was dedicated, Sen. Warner was in attendance. During the dedication luncheon, he told me that he often sees deer while driving around Virginia and asked whether he should just hit the deer or veer into the ditch. Being the researcher that I am and full of facts, I explained that the odds were dependent on the type of vehicle he was driving. Semi-truck drivers should always hit the deer, I explained, as well as SUV drivers. However, if you are driving a two-seater convertible, it depends.

The senator, slightly less patiently, asked simply, "Do I hit the deer or not?" Again, I began to explain the factors at play in such a situation, to which he replied "You aren't answering my question." As I began again, Gary Allen, a friend and colleague from the Virginia Department of Transportation, said "Hit the deer, Senator." That response satisfied the senator greatly, and he then went on to tell a fascinating story about when he was married to Elizabeth Taylor (a story for a different book, I suppose).

Tom (right) and Senator John Warner (left); photo
courtesy of VTTI

The point here is very similar to the point made earlier about *how* to crash when it is inevitable. While some deaths occur from a large animal coming through the windshield, most deaths occur when drivers depart the road to avoid hitting the animal. That is, the odds are in your favor if you stay on the road, in your lane, and hit the animal rather than veering off the road to avoid it. This is certainly true of opossums, skunks, squirrels, and even dogs and cats, although somewhat less so with moose. Now, this doesn't mean you shouldn't BRAKE LIKE HELL as I described previously. However, even when braking rapidly and as hard as you can, you should be at least a little wary of a secondary crash occurring if you are in traffic. Overall, though, stay in your lane unless you see a much better option like safely steering to a shoulder.

Defensive Driving 102:
Look and See

You can't be wary or aware if you don't know it's there!

As described in the intro to this book, VTTI has conducted many naturalistic driving studies that require putting tiny cameras, radar, and other sensors in people's own cars while they go about their everyday lives. We have data from enough cars, trucks, and motorcycles (about 4,000) over enough time (studies have lasted up to three years) to capture a lot of crashes and minor collisions (more than 1,500 and counting).

Having watched many crashes in the resulting naturalistic driving videos, one thing I can tell you is that the most common crash occurrence has at least two key ingredients present to make our figurative cake: The driver is not looking at the road, and something unexpected happens in front of the driver's car. There are often other elements at play, but these two factors combined are very common in a crash. I will talk at some length about the risks of taking your eyes off of the road, but I wanted to bring it up here in the context of defensive driving. So, here are a few tips to help you avoid crashes:

1. It's not just a matter of looking; you need to be able to see...far enough.

    This is the concept of sight distance. That is, the distance in terms of both space and time that you can see when you look. And sight distance changes all of the time due to traffic, weather, curves and hills, vegetation, etc. Get used to paying attention to not only how far you can see, but how fast things might change.

    I'll give you an example of an intersection near my house. When I stop at the stop sign, I need to make a left-hand turn, but the sight distance to the right is very short, the speeds are relatively high (about 45 mph), and there are often trucks headed to the local rock quarry. I literally have to make sure there is no traffic to the left and stare to the right as I pull out, prepared to hit the gas if needed. If I did a normal right-left, right-left look like they teach you in Driver's Ed class, I would have been mowed over a time or two by now by a 10-wheeled dump truck.

2. Look far down the road and plan ahead.

    Relative to sight distance, use whatever you have. If you can see far ahead, look far ahead. As with most aspects in life, there is an exception to this rule: You need to be wary of closer objects like parked cars, pedestrians, etc., particularly if you are traveling in an urban area. However, you still want to shift your gaze to look ahead in this environment to the extent feasible. Look ahead and through the windows/windshields of other vehicles for brake lights. This strategy allows you to make maneuvers such as braking or changing lanes without any sudden moves, thus helping you avoid conflicts with other vehicles. It also helps you avoid getting trapped behind cars on the highway.

3. Just because you don't see it doesn't mean it's not there.

If you look at crash databases, there is a factor in some crashes called "looked but failed to see." This factor is thought to be a key "cake" ingredient in roughly 10% of crashes. In these cases, the driver typically states that he or she looked in the direction necessary but didn't see the other vehicle or whatever else was coming. This may be because the driver went through the motions to look but wasn't really processing the information because he or she was thinking about something else, the driver's view was at least partially blocked by the structure of the car (maybe a blind spot), the object the driver hit wasn't very conspicuous (perhaps a bicycle rider in gray clothing traveling against a grayish background), and/or the driver was looking for something specific. You would be surprised at the number of cases in which a crash occurs because a driver was looking for a car and instead overlooked a truck, pulling out in front of the truck and hitting it. In any event, it is important to both look and see. Focus on looking hard and looking long enough to see anything that may be "hiding."

4. AHHH! Look out for the looming threshold.

Brake lights ahead convey the simple message that the driver has his or her foot on the brake. Most of the time, the driver is just resting his or her foot on the brake and is getting ready to slow, or is slowing gently. However, once in a while, the driver ahead is

photo courtesy of VTTI

slamming on the brakes. Unfortunately, the brake lights look the same regardless of the level of braking. If you are pretty close to the car, you may get other cues that the driver has slammed on the brakes. Notably, as you rapidly approach the stopping car, the visual angle (or, the size of the car in your visual field) gets larger pretty quickly. This is called "looming." At some distance away, you don't notice this looming because you are outside of what is called the "looming threshold," where the size of the car in your visual field does not change very fast. In such cases of being outside the looming threshold, you really can't tell the difference between a gentle brake and a hard brake maneuver. I have seen a number of crash cases during which Driver One looked away for a second or two when brake lights came on ahead, having assumed that Driver Two was applying a gentle brake. However, in these cases, Driver Two had slammed on his or her brakes; by the time Driver One looked back at the road, there was no time to stop. The moral of the story is that, if brake lights come on, keep looking until you know what the situation is and can react accordingly.

Defensive Driving 103: Watch Out!

Stay away from impaired drivers

I am using "impaired" in the broadest sense for this discussion, including being drowsy, distracted, drunk, and/or drugged. Not too many years ago, when you saw a car weaving out of the lane, chances were pretty good that you were witnessing a drunk driver. Now, you might be witnessing a texting driver, a driver checking stock on his or her smartphone, or a driver falling asleep at the wheel. The symptoms are mostly the same, but they should tell you one thing: Be aware of who is doing what, be wary, and stay away!

The most obvious indicator of an impaired driver is an inability to keep his/her vehicle in the travel lane. Beyond that, you should look for signs of the degree of impairment. If the offending driver is weaving a little out of the lane to the right onto an open shoulder, it could just be a momentary distraction and the driver is otherwise sober. If the offending driver is weaving in both directions and appears to be overcorrecting, or the driver is weaving more than a couple of feet out of the lane, or if you see such behavior exhibited two or more times during the span of just a few minutes, then you are driving near a hazard. You need to go out of your way to avoid this hazard.

Other, less obvious impaired behaviors include an inability to maintain speed. Drivers who continually speed up and slow down are typically impaired in some form. Also, watch out for inappropriate speeds that include drivers traveling too fast or too slow beyond what is reasonable.

Avoiding impaired drivers is a tip that can save your life. If you don't believe me, I will give you a statistic that should scare the hell out of you:

***More than 13% of drivers involved in fatal crashes* have invalid licenses or no license.**

In the good ol' U.S. of A., it's not easy to get your license revoked. Far and away, the easiest and most common way to lose your license is to get a DUI. However, engaging in other reckless behaviors, such as getting a second or third reckless driving conviction, will get you there as well. In any event, you should always watch other drivers and be wary.

General Resources

http://www.nhtsa.gov/Aggressive

http://www.nhtsa.gov/FARS

https://learningcenter.statefarm.com/safety-2/auto-2/watch-out-for-animals-in-the-road/

http://safety.transportation.org/htmlguides/DDD/Section01.htm

http://www.distraction.gov/downloads/pdfs/the-100-car-naturalistic-driving-study.pdf

https://www.aaafoundation.org/sites/default/files/UnlicensedToKillResearchUpdate.pdf

http://www.distraction.gov/downloads/pdfs/driver-distraction-commercial-vehicle-operations.pdf

http://www.ttnews.com/articles/basetemplate.aspx?storyid=37287&t=Crash-Death-Rate-Declines

http://consumerist.com/2015/01/23/nhtsa-to-suggest-but-not-require-sensor-enabled-brakes-for-all-new-vehicles/

Mollenhauer, M., Dingus, T., Carney, C., Hankey, J., & Jahns, S. (1997). Anti-lock brake systems: An assessment of training on driver effectiveness. *Accident Analysis & Prevention, 29*(1), 97-108. doi:10.1016/S0001-4575(96)00065-6

Hankey, J. M., McGehee, D. V., Dingus, T. A., Mazzae, E. N., & Garrott, W. R. (1996). Initial driver avoidance behavior and reaction time to an unalerted intersection incursion. In *Proceedings of the Human Factors and Ergonomics Society Annual Meeting, 40*(18), 896-899. doi:10.1177/154193129604001806

Chapter 4.

Adapt, Overcome, and Survive

Drivers adapt all of the time to try to manage their *perceived* risks. Sometimes they do so consciously, sometimes not. For example, when drivers accustomed to inclement weather slow down on icy roads, they slow down—or adapt—because they know that the risk is higher due to less friction on the road. However, drivers in Atlanta don't slow down during icy conditions, or don't slow down enough because they are unfamiliar with the risk and cannot judge it accurately. This is what happened in January 2014, when enough drivers in Atlanta failed to adapt to icy conditions and crashed, closing major roadways for several days.

The unfortunate part is that drivers are not only poor at judging their risks while driving, they often aren't very good at adapting, either. This simply means that they aren't changing their driving behavior—for instance, by slowing down—when the conditions call for it. VTTI studies have shown that:

Roughly 10% of drivers create between 40% and 50% of the overall crash risk.

A big part of this statistic is that these drivers don't know how or choose not to adapt. It's a mind-boggling fact, but it's true. Therefore, it is important that you, your family, kids, friends, and dogs not only avoid being among the 10% but know how to watch out for those 10%!

There are folks participating in the VTTI naturalistic driving studies who illustrate this point. We have seen drivers in three-year studies who never had a near-crash, or close call. By contrast, we have seen drivers in one-year studies experience several dozen near-crashes and seven crashes or minor collisions. These latter drivers have interesting habits, such as removing a tongue stud while simultaneously talking on a handheld phone and driving 70 mph (for those of you who may not know, it takes both hands to remove a tongue stud). Or driving while eating…with chopsticks. Or having the passenger hold the wheel while lighting a two-foot bong.

These 10% of drivers, or at least the portion who do not have a death wish, obviously have issues gauging perceived and actual risks. But lest ye have never been sitting in a ditch next to an icy road, or climbed sheepishly out of a car explaining why you didn't stop in time, or had to make up a story about the inadequacies of speed limit signs, do not cast the first stone upon your brethren. Because, as you will learn, driving risk is very complex indeed. I have studied driving safety for more than 30 years and still have much to learn, as do my numerous bright colleagues.

In effect, we all adapt at times when we drive. And adaptation can be both good (if you adapted to maintain a low level of risk) and bad (if you didn't adapt enough or if you didn't perceive the change in risk).

Below are suggestions about how to minimize your risk and adapt accordingly to different scenarios.

Adaptation 101

Road and traffic conditions

Being able to adapt appropriately to changing conditions and capabilities is key to minimizing your risk, probably as much as any aspect of safe driving.

The kind of road that you drive on has a big impact on your risk. Roads are much safer than they were just 15 or 20 years ago, and they are getting better all of the time. Better sight distances, wide shoulders, interchanges instead of intersections, lighting in key locations, better markings, and "roadside hardware" that includes different types of barriers and guardrails; these have all made a real difference in road safety. There are big changes in risk based on the type of road on which you are traveling. For example:

You are *2.4 times more likely* (odds = 2.4) to get in a crash on a two-lane road than on a divided highway.

This is a form of exposure where you can control your risk by driving on safer roads, such as interstates and divided highways. However, you don't often have control over the roads you drive unless you have alternative routes available. If you do have choices, in general, pick roads that have the features described above to minimize your risk. However, I have chosen not to talk extensively about this point because, more often than not, you have to "dance with who you brung" in terms of the roads you are traveling to get from Point A to Point B. What will perhaps help you control your risk more is your ability to *adapt* successfully to whatever kind of road you travel.

My wife, Melissa (the one on the left of the car trunk in the photo below), and I met in graduate school. We were working in the same lab, doing driving safety research with our advisor, Walt Wierwille, who was a pioneer in our field for aspects such as steering control, drowsiness, and visual attention. Melissa still works at VTTI. That's right, we have fascinating conversations around the dinner table, particularly about injurious crashes. Which reminds me of a conversation I once had with a paramedic. When I asked him "How is business?" he responded "It's dead, but it's picking up…"

from the author's personal photo collection

Anyway, Melissa's master's thesis was a study in which she characterized the attention required to drive on different kinds of roads, including rural curvy two-lane, straight two-lane, four-lane, and divided highways. She and I measured parameters like sight distance, road width, shoulder width, obstacle presence, posted speeds, etc. What she found is that different road types require different levels of attention. Interstates require less attention than rural roads. This was not surprising; the surprising part was *the degree to which* different roads require different levels of attention. You have to keep your eyes on a curvy roadway just to keep your car on the road.

By contrast, if you're traveling on an interstate, you can take your eyes off of the road for a relatively longer amount of time (which still isn't long) and keep your vehicle in your travel lane. Of course, taking your eyes off of the interstate won't help you avoid hitting something in your lane.

The point here is that you need to make sure you adapt to the road you are traveling to maintain a low risk. In this case, things like engaging in secondary tasks or looking at an external object or event of interest should wait until the road demand is low, such as while at a stop sign. You can also slow down, which is a good strategy as long as you are not going too slow or unexpectedly slow to the point where you impede the flow of traffic. To keep yourself safe while driving, you need to be wary and adapt more than you may think necessary.

Another important aspect that requires adaptation includes traffic stability. When traffic is light and free-flowing:

You are roughly *one-half as likely* (odds = 0.5) to get in a crash as when roads are congested and traffic is unstable.

One thing to note is that, if traffic is congested to the point where it is moving slowly, you are less likely to get injured since you are traveling at a lower speed. Why? Because the driver can adapt to very heavy traffic more successfully when slowdowns are more expected. An important aspect here is the stability of traffic. Traffic that slows and speeds up numerous times leads to more crashes. The best way to adapt overall is to keep your eyes on the road.

When they were in high school, my son, Chris, and his friend, Nick, were taking a three-hour trip back home from a concert. They ran into heavy traffic on the highway, and it got to the point where it was moving pretty slowly. My son was taking a nap in the passenger seat while Nick was driving a shift. Being the conscientious friend that Nick was, he was listening to music on his iPod through his earbuds so Chris could sleep.

Well, a typical crash ingredient became present: Nick looked down momentarily at his iPod, traffic stopped, and Nick hit the car in front. The unexpected had become more likely, and the key ingredients combined to make our figurative cake. No one was hurt, but damage was done to the car. At that point, the issue from my perspective was that they were traveling *in Chris' car*. So, there was an insurance claim, which Nick paid for in full. No harm, no foul, except that Nick remained on my policy for a couple of years afterwards, despite our efforts to explain to the insurance company that he was not a family member or primary driver of the car.

As illustrated above and time and time again, the most common type of crash occurs when an unexpected event happens while the driver is looking away from the road for any reason, including internal or external distraction, fatigue, or just looking around. Another key ingredient is when the chance of something unexpected happening increases because of road or traffic conditions, so adapt accordingly by being alert and wary. You can also decrease your risk of a crash and be able to look away from the road *a **little** longer* by increasing your space and time, meaning the headway or following distance.

Driving in bad weather

Driving in bad weather (rain, snow, fog, sleet, freezing rain) increases your risk of a crash due to reduced visibility and/or reduced traction. As a rule of thumb:

Bad weather *increases your risk of a crash between 70% and 80%* when both visibility and traction are impacted.

A great way to avoid such risk is to stay home when the weather is bad, if you can. That doesn't mean I'm advocating staying home if it's drizzling outside. Let's just say that, if your local law enforcement and weather forecaster say to avoid travel due to inclement weather, heed their advice if you possibly can.

Almost every year, in some state somewhere, there is a huge pileup on a foggy interstate. This is a prime example of when traction isn't bad but visibility is terrible. It's also a prime example of violating a driver's expectations, which is a recurring theme in this book. It turns out that, in several common crash scenarios, violating others' expectations on the road is one of those key ingredients present to make our figurative cake.

In a nutshell, drivers don't really expect to see stopped cars on the interstate, so they often don't adapt enough to that possibility, even in heavy fog. If you think about a 50- or 60-car/truck pileup, a significant number of those drivers didn't expect vehicles to be stopped. Therefore, those drivers didn't adapt enough to the fact that they couldn't see. At VTTI, we have a test track called the Smart Road, on which we can make fog (and rain, snow, and ice). We often get a call to do some fog research aimed at trying to slow people down when they can't see. My friend and colleague, Ron Gibbons, conducts a lot of this visibility research. Based on that research, I have four pieces of advice if you find yourself in a very low visibility situation:

1. Slow down, thinking about how far you can really see and how long it takes your car to stop. You don't want to drive faster than you can see to stop. As you will learn throughout this book, this means going slower than you probably thought necessary to make a stop.

2. Focus on the road ahead. Actively search for any signs of cars ahead, even though it is not particularly pleasant to stare into a uniform scene of fog or snow. Don't get distracted, and don't look away from the road.

3. Turn on your lights, typically on low beam. This helps you see a bit better, but it also makes you more conspicuous to drivers behind you.

4. Don't become a target that others can't see. In general, stay out of the left lane. If you are going really slow or need to stop, turn on your emergency hazards to increase conspicuity for those traveling behind you. Consider moving over to the shoulder if you can, at least until traffic backs up well behind you.

Fog production on the Smart Road at VTTI; photo by Rick Griffiths

Momentum is your best friend
and your worst enemy

The other part of the bad weather equation is traction.

My first job out of college was working as a human factors engineer for a large aerospace company. I lived in the mountains of Colorado and commuted each day down the aforementioned Highway 285 to the suburbs just west of Denver. For those of you who haven't experienced living and commuting at a high altitude, concepts like "southern exposure" are very important when you live at 9,000 feet. It mostly meant that my house had snow around it until the end of May, while my neighbor across the street was enjoying bright, spring-like weather in mid-March because he faced south. It also meant that I had plenty of winter driving in which I could both participate and observe, in combination with big uphill and downhill stretches.

One particular behavior stands out from those days. Many of the commuters along Highway 285 had big pickups with oversized tires and four-wheel drive. Those features were admittedly very handy. The knobby tires and extra drive wheels allowed drivers to get through a lot of slick spots and deep snow.

What always amazed me, though, was the misconception that those trucks stopped faster or steered better than any other car or truck traveling at highway speeds while going downhill on an icy road. If you think about it, even a two-wheel-drive car or truck has brakes on all four wheels. And a newer car has anti-locking brake systems (ABS) and maybe even electronic stability control (ESC).

The point is, ground clearance and four-wheel drive do not help you stop on ice more than any other vehicle. This is why, during my Highway 285 ventures, I often came across four-wheel-drive trucks stuck in the median, against the guardrail, or in the ditch. A good day was when they were still "shiny side up."

When traction is low, you have to think a lot about momentum. Momentum is the quantity of motion of a moving object, all mathematically defined as mass (weight) times speed. This essentially means that, if you are driving in a straight line on very slick roads, your vehicle will tend to keep going straight and remain at the same speed. Steering and braking are much less effective in such a scenario because the traction is so low that the tires don't grip to exert much force, even if you have a four-wheel-drive truck.

This means that you have to do everything ahead of time and in slow motion during bad weather. In general, you want to control momentum by driving much slower, particularly if the roads are icy. If you are coming to a stop sign, for example, the slower speed in this scenario will help you safely maneuver to a stop in the right place and not 20 feet into the intersection. Planning ahead will also help you: Begin braking gently much farther in advance than you normally would to avoid skidding. If you are going downhill, drive even slower and begin to slow down even farther in advance because gravity is working to literally pull you down the hill. The same is true with making a turn: Brake gently way ahead of the turn and slow way down before you have to turn. If you wait too long and brake or steer in the curve at too high of a speed in bad weather, you will go straight, no matter what you do with the steering wheel.

We have all heard this, but the next time it's icy, take the family to a big parking lot and practice, practice, practice all of these driving scenarios! Stop as fast as you can, feeling the beautiful chatter of your ABS and how the vehicle reacts on a slick surface; spin out and correct a slide; practice stopping at the right spot.

Of course, the other side of the momentum equation is when you want more momentum because you are stuck and can't get your vehicle moving ahead. In this case, you want to both generate and conserve momentum to keep moving. In essence, you want just enough momentum, but not too much! Since this is a safety book, I need to remind you of this obvious fact because it makes driving on ice even trickier. For example, when you are going up a hill on ice, you want to start with a run-and-go at the bottom of the hill. In these conditions, however, you have to switch very quickly from conservatively generating momentum to getting rid of momentum at the crest of the hill.

Similar to the case of a disabled vehicle, the following piece of advice applies to winter driving: If you get stuck in a travel lane, get out of the car, and get to a safe spot on the shoulder. The tendency to want to push the car is only a good idea if you are sure you are not going to be squished by the next car that also just happens to be traveling on ice!

Bad weather is clearly a time when you need to adapt appropriately to the conditions. Remember, the risk of a fatal or injurious crash is much higher during bad weather. Some of this risk is due to traction and momentum, but a large component of this increased risk is also visibility. So, again, ADAPT! Stay engaged in the driving task, keep your eyes on the road, and slow down when traction or visibility is limited.

Adaptation 102

When your car is not your car

Another friend and colleague, Mike Perel (shown in the photo on the next page), worked for the National Highway Traffic Safety Administration (NHTSA) for more than 40 years until he retired a few years ago. Mike participated in many, many studies during those years. One that was particularly unique and important to this nar-

Tom is flanked by former NHTSA researchers Mike Perel (left) and Mike Goodman (right) during a congressional testimony; photo courtesy of VTTI

rative involved identifying the risk of driving an unfamiliar car or motorcycle. Mike and NHTSA found that, if you are unfamiliar with the car you are driving (that is, if you have less than 500 miles of experience driving the vehicle):

You are *two to three times more likely* (odds = 2.0 – 3.0) to get in a crash compared to driving a car with which you are familiar.

This risk, of course, applies to new cars, rental cars, and borrowed cars. However, this fact is becoming more relevant as we enter an era when ride/car sharing is becoming increasingly popular. This statistic also applies to motorcycles, which have the same or even a greater risk level.

There are at least two factors at play here. First, different vehicles sometimes have pretty different handling and braking characteristics.

The more differences among the vehicles, such as a compact car versus an SUV, the greater the risk when you first start driving an unfamiliar vehicle. I have seen a number of cases during which someone gets into a crash or near-crash because they were driving a friend's SUV when they had pretty much only driven small cars in the past.

The second factor has to do with unfamiliar controls. You don't have to drive too many different cars before you start pulling out your hair trying to figure out how to turn on the damned windshield wipers when it starts to pour down rain. If you're like me, you don't even have to look past your own driveway to find several vehicles with different controls that present limitless frustration. If you add in all of the unfamiliar controls, you start to realize that you just spent the better part of a minute looking around trying to figure out how to find your favorite classic rock or alternative station in a desperate attempt to get Justin Bieber out of your head.

The problem with unfamiliarity is almost certainly worse among motorcycles, simply because they vary in many different ways. I talk about this in a later chapter, but the difference in horsepower between a Harley Electra Glide and a Suzuki GSX-R is almost triple! Motorcycles are completely different animals; other than (mostly) having two wheels, they don't have much else in common among themselves.

So…adapt! Give yourself and your unfamiliar vehicle more space and time. Be overly cautious in turns and corners. Act like you work on a reptile farm (that is, make no sudden moves) by planning ahead. In addition, take a minute or two to figure out how the most important controls work in the car you're driving, such as lights and windshield wipers. Set the temperature before you put the car in gear so that you will be comfortable, and set up the stereo so that you are good to go, before you go!

Adaptation 103

When you are not yourself

Adaptation is one of the real keys to reducing your crash risk. As you've read, driving is highly dynamic: The roads, road conditions, traffic conditions, and even vehicles are constantly changing, and you need to change in turn by reducing your speed, staying more focused, etc.

The other dynamic part of the adaptation equation is *you*. Sometimes you are a better, more capable, and more engaged driver than at other times. I believe that a key to avoiding crashes is understanding those times during which you are disengaged from the primary task of driving and to modify your behavior accordingly. Here are some tips and advice on doing so:

1. If you have been drinking (within the legal limit and even well below, I hope), taking prescription medication, smoking marijuana, and/or have some kind of other impairment, let someone else drive if you have the option.

   However, if you feel you need to drive, you need to adapt. Adapt before you drive by *not* doing whatever it is you are doing for a good, long while prior to leaving. Essentially, leave later when you are in a more alert and sober state. During your drive, adapting means driving slower, minimizing any distractions, focusing on staying engaged in driving, and avoiding areas with heavy traffic and vulnerable road users such as pedestrians or bicyclists.

2. If you are experiencing serious stress, your driving ability will likely be impaired. Studies have shown that drivers under interpersonal, marital, vocational, and/or financial stress:

Are *nearly four times more likely* (odds = 4.0) to be involved in a crash than those who are not under such stress.

Big sources of stress can include tragedies in your life, such as the death of a spouse or other family member, divorce or marital separation, or a serious illness. Stress factors can also include positive changes, such as marriage, pregnancy, retirement, or a new home purchase. It is important to be aware of these changes and how they affect your driving. If you know of someone going through a tough time or a life-changing event, offer to drive them. If you are the one experiencing a stressful time, focus on staying engaged in driving, take extra time to get to your destination, stop more often during a long trip, drive slower and leave more time and space around you, or simply remove yourself from the driving task and ask a friend or family member to drive.

3. Adapt over the long term.

   Maintaining mobility is vitally important for those of the aging population. Such mobility will also become more vitally important to society as the overall population ages during the next 25 years. A key to maintaining this mobility is to adapt to your changes in capability. Fortunately, older drivers tend to do a good job of adapting for a long time. I'll discuss senior driver issues later in the book, so look for more key points in that chapter.

General Resources

http://www.nhtsa.gov/FARS

http://www.sciencedirect.com/science/article/pii/S0966692309000702

http://ntl.bts.gov/lib/33000/33300/33359/33359.pdf

http://bit.ly/1MaZKId

Hulse, M. C., Dingus, T. A., Fischer, T., & Wierwille, W. W. (1989). The influence of roadway parameters on driver perception of attentional demand. In A. Mital (Ed.), *Advances in Industrial Ergonomics and Safety I*, 451-456. New York: Taylor & Francis.

Chapter 5.

Do Not Mix Mind-altering Substances with Driving

It's a no-brainer that alcohol increases a driver's risk. With more and more states legalizing marijuana, there is also an obvious discussion to be had about this substance and relative potential risks behind the wheel. But there are other impairing factors that drivers face, ones you may not automatically consider.

Battle of the Sexes

I often ask my transportation safety classes and other groups: "What is the most dangerous, mind-altering substance when it comes to driving?" Almost invariably, they say "alcohol." Sometimes I get an occasional answer of "LSD" or "shrooms" in my college classes, although I am not sure that those answers come from a scientific source. Interestingly, marijuana is invariably missing as a dangerous substance relative to driving. I will talk about that later, but I believe it is because it is hard to get in a crash while sitting on your couch eating cheese puffs.

However, when all factors are considered, I believe that the most dangerous mind-altering substance is testosterone. Who has the most testosterone? Young males. Who are the riskiest drivers by a wide margin? Young males. Notice I said "riskiest" and not "worst." Many young males will argue fervently against this claim, in my opinion largely because they are laden with testosterone. As young males most often do, they will talk about performance criteria, such as reaction time or an ability to take curves faster or their ability to drive in snow. Unfortunately, performance and skill do not matter as much in reducing crash risk as JUDGMENT.

Young males are more prone to make errors in judgment by:

- Driving faster;
- Driving with shorter headways (or, tailgating);
- Engaging in distracting tasks more often, such as texting;

- Engaging in distracting tasks at the worse possible times (intersections, taking curves, etc.); and
- Driving impaired due to alcohol.

I should mention that there are few, if any, gender differences when it comes to *driving ability*. This is not true of driver judgment, however. While young females may also undertake some of these bad driving habits, they do so less often as a population. Still, if you are a female and you *choose* to engage in these risky behaviors, you will be at just as much risk as your male counterparts.

Dude, Where's My Car?

Driving over the legal alcohol limit is always a bad idea. Alcohol reduces inhibition, increases self-confidence, makes one more susceptible to social influence, reduces attention, promotes secondary task engagement, and reduces reaction time. All of these traits are bad for driving, which is why:

Your odds of being in a fatal crash at the legal blood alcohol content (BAC) limit of 0.08% are *about seven times higher* (odds = 7.0) than driving sober.

For my daughter, who is 105 pounds soaking wet, that means no more than two glasses (5 oz.) of wine in an hour. For me (a svelte 185 pounds…or so), that means no more than four beers in an hour, and then no more than one beer every hour after that. At a BAC above 0.08%, the odds climb to very high levels:

At about twice the legal limit (0.15% BAC), your odds of being in a fatal crash skyrocket *300 to 600 times higher* (odds = 300.0 – 600.0), depending on your age and gender.

Never, never, never let anyone drive a car who is in this kind of shape. A BAC of 0.15% essentially means doubling the above alcohol allowance numbers for my daughter and me (that is, four servings for her in an hour, and eight for me). If you are younger, you are at greater risk of a fatal crash at an increased BAC level. If you are female, you are at greater risk of a fatal crash at an increased BAC level, marking the only time in this book that females experience an increased risk relative to their male counterparts. Most of these risks represent the death of *the driver*. With any luck at all, you will just kill your fool self and no one else while driving under the influence. If you kill someone else, it only gets worse.

Now to some other issues relative to driving under the influence of alcohol…

Another pop quiz: Is it better to take 1,000 cab rides home or drive drunk once and end up with a DUI? They cost the same. Think about it. For most folks, that equates to a lifetime of being chauffeured around in an impaired state. For example, if you decide to drink heavily once per week away from home, you can take a cab home for the next *20 years* for the cost of one DUI. How can you tell if you need a cab? You can get a free BAC calculator

from the author's personal photo collection

app for your smartphone, or you can buy a cheap pocket Breathalyzer. You can even calculate your BAC in your head; the only complicating factors are portion size and alcohol content (think strong beers). But the moral of the story is, just don't drive drunk. Period.

Around our small college town, we have what is known as DUI-Guy. DUI-Guy is typically a male between the ages of 20 and 40, riding a 49.5 cc motor scooter. You can kind of think that, well okay, this guy is concerned about the environment or trying to save money on gas. Until you pass the same guy in a rainstorm, or in the winter on icy roads. Then you think, well, this guy obviously has been convicted of driving under the influence of alcohol, and the only way he can get around is on a scooter because it doesn't require a driver's license, license plate, or insurance. It is interesting that a huge portion of DUI-Guys wear a full face helmet. Do you think it's because they are super safe or because they don't want anyone to know who they are? I'll let you be the judge.

The good news about DUI-Guy is that he probably didn't kill or injure someone while driving drunk (think vehicular homicide). Obviously, he's not in county lockup with a conscience full of the person or persons he injured or killed, every day, for the rest of his life.

There is a really important point here. Even with all of the DUI penalties and improved enforcement:

***One-third of the fatalities* in the U.S. still involve alcohol.**

Stay home, take a cab, or get someone sober to drive you home.

Just Because You Can, Doesn't Mean You Should: Part 1

This first installment of "Just Because You Can" is aimed at those who choose to drive after drinking alcohol, even though you may be within the legal BAC limit. As a rule of thumb:

The odds of a fatal crash double (odds = 2.0) **with every BAC of 0.02%.**

That is essentially one drink for most of us; with two drinks, the odds double again. Those odds are still higher for young drivers. Essentially, driving at half of the legal limit (BAC = 0.04%):

Puts you at *four times the risk* (odds = 4.0) compared to driving sober.

Those are really high odds. That's why some countries, like Germany, have set their legal BAC limit at 0.05% for adults. So, get the most sober person to drive home, or take a cab.

Our friends at the National Highway Traffic Safety Administration (NHTSA) recently published an excellent study that estimated the crash risk for differing BAC levels. These risk estimates are shown in the table below. One thing that you have to understand about this table is that it considers a sample for all police-reported crashes, *not just fatal crashes*. This is important because, as you can tell, the numbers below are different than the ones highlighted above. This is certainly because the crashes included are different; it may also be because the data are more recent.

A couple of items to note here. At very low levels of alcohol (for instance, one drink or less), the odds appear to be protective, or less than 1.0. Here is another quiz: Why do you

BrAC Relative Risk Unadjusted and Adjusted for Age and Gender

BrAC	Unadjusted Risk	Adjusted Risk (Age and Gender)
0.00	1.00	1.00
0.01	0.51	0.54
0.02	0.82	0.85
0.03	1.17	1.20
0.04	1.57	1.60
0.05	2.05	2.07
0.06	2.61	2.61
0.07	3.25	3.22
0.08	3.98	3.93
0.09	4.83	4.73
0.10	5.79	5.64
0.11	6.88	6.67
0.12	8.11	7.82
0.13	9.51	9.11
0.14	11.07	10.56
0.15	12.82	12.18
0.16	14.78	13.97
0.17	16.97	15.96
0.18	19.40	18.17
0.19	22.09	20.60
0.20+	25.08	23.29

Note: (Relative to BrAC = .00)

from National Highway Traffic Safety Administration. (2015). *Traffic Safety Facts: Drug and Alcohol Crash Risk* (DOT HS 812 117).

think that is? Well, it certainly appears that drivers are ADAPTING to the low alcohol levels, probably because they know they have had a drink and are thus driving a little more conservatively. Good for them!

However, the risk starts climbing at a BAC of 0.03%, with risk increasing significantly beginning around a BAC of 0.04%. Again, depending on your weight and gender, that is just a drink or two during the course of an hour.

I'm realistic, though. There's a good chance most of you will forget these increased odds after a night out with friends or when you feel like you don't have any other choice but to drive. But never, never, never drive while over the legal alcohol limit. Even if you are going to drive after a glass or two of wine, I recommend focusing on ADAPTING, as discussed in the previous section. That means driving slower, paying closer attention, leaving long headways. Avoid areas with pedestrians. In other words, focus on minimizing risk.

Sometimes You Should Stay Home and Eat Your Cheese Puffs

Marijuana has been around for a long time. When I was in college in the 1970s, my roommate, Rick, and I used to smoke weed and eat an entire Pepperidge Farm Coconut Cake. We would walk to the grocery store and pick one up and eat it on the way back. It was *frozen* but was meant to be thawed; it just never got to the point where it thawed. I wonder why…

There is an important point to this story: When you get to the point where you want to eat half a frozen cake before it thaws, you might be impaired enough that you don't need to drive. Fortunately, Rick and I were not motivated to drive during these outings, and we could walk. I am guessing that, if we were not close enough to walk, we would have just stayed home and eaten brown sugar out of the bag. Despite the fact that marijuana has been around for a long time, we don't know a whole lot about how it affects driving. We know that at *some* level there is *significant* impairment, but there hasn't been a lot of work into marijuana and driving primarily because it has been illegal and the research is pretty hard to perform. Of course, that is all changing with the legalization of medicinal and recreational marijuana in several states and our nation's capital, with more states certainly to follow.

So, here we are: We don't know what the legal marijuana limit should be. Even if we did know, we don't have an effective road-side test to measure it, and we don't really know how it interacts with fatigue and other drugs such as alcohol. For example, let's say you consumed alcohol but are below the legal BAC limit— maybe 0.05%, or two to three beers depending on your weight. If you were also smoking pot, we don't know if you are in worse shape at that point as a driver compared to consuming a fourth beer that would have put you over the legal BAC limit.

Of course, there are talking heads who will claim that we're already seeing an increase in crashes due to the legalization of marijuana in some states. A relatively quick Internet search for "increased crashes marijuana" is going to bring you to several reports that seem to verify such a statement. However, there are contradictory findings, such as a recent study that shows the injury/crash rate at lower levels in Colorado since the legalization of recreational pot.

In February 2015, NHTSA released results from a study that sought to determine the crash risk of drug- and alcohol-impaired driving compared to a control group of drivers. This particular study put the odds of a crash risk while under the influence of marijuana, for example, between 1.00 and 1.05. Drivers who tested positive for any legal or illegal drugs but no alcohol saw odds of 1.02.

It should be noted that all of these studies most certainly tested the bloodstream for the active ingredient in marijuana, THC. The issue here is:

1. The THC level doesn't necessarily correlate well with how impaired your driving is.

2. Unlike alcohol, THC remains in your bloodstream for a very long time, even days or weeks. (This is, of course, why football players and others need "wizzinators" to pass a drug test for marijuana.)

Essentially, at least some drivers tested in the NHTSA study could have been stoned *three days prior* and still tested positive for THC. Obviously, the driver is not still impaired at this point yet is classified as "drug positive" in the results. This is undoubtedly why the odds are closer than one might expect to a risk of 1.0. Don't get me wrong, the NHTSA study makes a great contribution, but it highlights my point that we still have a long way to go to understand the risks of marijuana and driving.

At this stage, one thing is certain: We don't have enough good, real-world data to set and enforce a reasonable marijuana limit. You are going to hear media reports for a long time that say it's both highly dangerous and not dangerous at all. (There are a few examples of these varied reports listed as general resources at the end of this chapter. Make sure you read the intro and epilogue of this book to learn about transportation safety data reported by the media.)

There are many questions about marijuana use that will take a long time to answer. If you are a policymaker, please fund my marijuana and driving research (just kidding…sort of). Honestly, we do need good studies with crash data, but they will take time to develop. We need a large-scale, long-term naturalistic driving study to understand how the causal and contributing factors of crashes change regarding marijuana use. And, yes, we need simulator and survey studies to conduct this research, as long as they are properly interpreted.

All of these research concepts should focus on such questions as: What happens when alcohol use is the primary impairment versus marijuana use as the primary impairment? Does marijuana lead to other risks, such as increased distraction or fatigue? It may sound funny, but over-adaptation and driving too slowly are possibilities with respect to marijuana.

Personally, I believe that drivers can adapt better to their driving state under the influence of marijuana than tequila! You don't typically see crashes occurring at more than 100 mph with marijuana impairment like you do with alcohol. And marijuana-impaired drivers probably don't drive aggressively in general. There is the old joke: Did you hear about the two stoners who bumped into each other and got into a fight in a bar? Of course not, they were too busy apologizing! It's easy enough to find advocates on both sides of the marijuana debate, but we just don't have all of the information available from the context of actual driving to make definitive statements about marijuana use in relation to driving. Because we have much to learn about this topic, I won't even be able to estimate your risk as of this writing. This will change in the next few years, so stay tuned.

I will, however, give you a couple of words of advice about how to approach the use of marijuana with respect to driving:

1. Treat marijuana like alcohol. Stay home, take a cab, or get someone else to drive.

2. Marijuana in 2015 is a strong drug. Don't underestimate it. It takes very little time or energy these days to get really stoned. Just a couple of puffs can really get you there. There are also many edible choices, and these can have both strong and long-lasting effects, even longer than alcohol. Plan accordingly if you take a trip to the "Green Planet" in Denver or the "Bulldog" in Amsterdam.

General Resources

http://www.bankrate.com/finance/personal-finance/dui-memorial-day-20-000-1.aspx

http://seattle.cbslocal.com/2014/02/04/study-fatal-car-crashes-involving-marijuana-have-tripled/

http://www.thedenverchannel.com/news/local-news/study-finds-100-percent-in-crease-in-fatal-pot-related-crashes-in-colorado

http://www.washingtonpost.com/news/the-watch/wp/2014/08/05/since-marijuana-legalization-highway-fatalities-in-colorado-are-at-near-historic-lows/

http://gatton.uky.edu/faculty/sandford/391_f13/marijuana.pdf

http://healthland.time.com/2011/12/02/why-medical-marijuana-laws-reduce-traffic-deaths/

http://www.jsad.com/doi/abs/10.15288/jsa.2000.61.387

National Highway Traffic Safety Administration. (2015). *Traffic Safety Facts: Drug and Alcohol Crash Risk* (DOT HS 812 117).

Chapter 6.

Be Attentive and Alert

Driving Drowsy

I was once in Key West watching the street performers down by the waterfront. One performer was commenting about the risk of his job as he was standing on top of an aluminum pole (not attached to anything) while juggling five flaming batons. He said he did not want to die as part of his risky performances but, instead, "wanted to die like my grandfather did; peacefully, in his sleep…not like his passengers."

Drowsy driving has long been known to be a source of impairment and crashes. For many years, we thought it was mostly a long-haul truck problem, with about *20% of truck crashes* having fatigue as a key ingredient in a crash, while light-vehicle crashes due to drowsy driving were in the range of 4% to 8%. Recently, however, there is a growing body of naturalistic and crash data that show fatigue is an all-vehicle problem, including cars, small trucks, and buses/motorcoaches. Specifically:

Crashes and near-crashes have drowsiness involvement *about 15% to 20% of the time.*

What these studies also show is that drowsiness is not limited to the wee hours of the morning, although that is certainly one peak time. Light-vehicle drivers suffer drowsiness symptoms during long morning commutes and in the early afternoon. Short-haul truck drivers (think beer or potato chip trucks) tend to be fatigued the most on Mondays, after experiencing some sleep loss over the weekend.

For long-haul trucks, the same trends hold true. That is, drowsiness can occur during all times of the day, with several peak times. VTTI researchers performed a study in the late 1990s that examined drowsiness for single and team long-haul drivers. The results showed that:

Pretty much any time of the day or night, *about 4% of truck drivers are falling asleep at the wheel.*

We're talking head-bobbing, eye-rubbing, truck-weaving types of falling asleep. That sounds like a pretty small percentage, until you begin to count the number of trucks you encounter on your next family vacation. The interstate nearest my house, I-81, has periods of the week/day during which traffic is more than 50% trucks. It is common for me to encounter more than 100 trucks during a four-hour drive to Washington, D.C. On average, such a trip puts me in close proximity every hour to a 40-ton vehicle where the driver is falling asleep at the wheel! It's a scary thought, but one more reason to **STAY AWAY FROM TRUCKS**. As mentioned previously, if you are going to pass a truck, risk the ticket and pass it briskly.

Regardless of the vehicle you drive, your crash risk:

Increases at least two times with any level of drowsiness **(odds = 2.0) and** *between four to 40 times* **(odds = 4.0 – 40.0) when you drive at a "moderately" drowsy level or higher, depending on how tired you are.**

In this case, a moderate drowsiness level is when you are beginning to struggle to stay awake, find yourself yawning, rubbing your face, and moving around in the seat more than normal. Another important symptom of drowsiness is what we call slow eyelid closures. Unlike a quick blink, a slow closure is like it sounds: The eyelid droops slowly over the eye and then is opened. If you experience slow eyelid closures and perhaps head nods, it is past time to find a safe place to pull over and rest. After all, it is hard to drive with your eyes closed.

The onset of drowsiness is something that can be useful to understand. For my master's thesis, I studied drowsiness, alcohol, and the combination thereof with the help of my advisor, Walt Wierwille, and lab mate, Lenora Hardee. Our goal was to try to develop algorithms that detected when a driver first became drowsy and to warn such drivers via a chime and "tell-tale" icon on the dash that it was time to take a break. The study found that the pattern of sleep onset came in "bouts" of drowsiness lasting a few minutes, followed by a period during which the drivers were able to wake themselves up for a little while. Even though our drivers were sleep deprived, the first bout of drowsiness did not occur for about 15 or 20 minutes. With each successive bout of drowsiness, though, the amount of recovery time declined, and the time between bouts became shorter. These symptoms characterize what we call *sleep inertia*. Simply stated, a body needs sleep. While you can delay the onset of drowsiness for a little while with coffee, energy drinks, conversation, music, and cold air, the urge and need for sleep will overwhelm those small arousing influences sooner rather than later.

How do you combat sleep inertia and decrease your risk associated with drowsy driving?

Take a good nap

There really is only one thing that you can do when sleep inertia begins to build: Take a nap! Alternatively, you can switch drivers if you have someone more alert willing to take the wheel. The key here is to make sure the alternative driver actually is more alert.

My good friends, Bob and Rick, once traveled across country to Boston. Because Bob was often distracted by other interesting events, they started driving at midnight. Rick started driving because Bob had just been at a party, and Bob was asleep in the back. As Bob recalled, dawn was just breaking when he was woken from his slumber by the sound of the car hitting gravel and Rick muttering that he couldn't stay awake anymore. Rick pulled over to let Bob take the wheel. Bob said he was fine, although he was clearly in the process of waking up. Rick climbed into the back of the car, and off they went.

About 15 minutes later, Bob was enjoying the nice, warm sun on the car...a little too much. As Bob said, it was like the scene in "National Lampoon's Vacation" when all the Griswolds were asleep in the Truckster, including Clark, who was the driver.

Well, Bob quickly woke up when he mowed into a small pole, and he yanked the wheel and jammed on the brakes, sending the car into a 360-degree spin. Rick was snapped out of his dreams by the sound of the squealing tires, sitting up just in time to catch the flash of an abutment passing by. They managed to come to a halt pointing in the right direction, so Bob dropped the car into first gear and started driving again. Apparently, Rick didn't agree that Bob was fit to continue driving, so they changed shifts again. They both made it to their destination, wide awake and ready for action. The point here is that the nap you take has to overcome the sleep inertia, meaning you need to allot time for both the nap and to wake up!

More and more folks these days suffer from sleep disorders, such as sleep apnea. Many of you may have sleep apnea and be unaware that you do. If you are a male, one quick way to tell if you may be at risk of sleep apnea is to measure your neck size. If it is 17 inches or more, there is a good chance you have sleep apnea. If you snore a lot or people tell you it sounds like you quit breathing when you snore, you may have sleep apnea. If any of this sounds familiar, go see your doctor for appropriate treatments. Of course, there are also the garden-variety insomniacs like me who spend hours awake in the middle of the night thinking about how to write a book…

In any event, the important point here is that, for some, sleep inertia can come on quick and hard. So, pay attention to your alertness level, take a nap when you need it, and get to your destination in one piece with no scratches on your car (or worse!).

Engaged Driving (or, Pay Attention!)

Our friends at State Farm recently convened a panel of experts to write a series of papers about engaged driving. In this sense, engaged driving simply means staying focused on driving and avoiding distraction. My friend, former student, and colleague, Charlie Klauer, who heads up the VTTI teen driving research, participated in this State Farm panel with me. I wrote a paper based on results from four of our naturalistic driving studies that focused on adults, teens, trucks, and cell phone use. Some odds from this paper are included later.

These studies showed that, in general, the presence of distraction as a key ingredient to all types of crashes has been underestimated for many years, similarly to the way drowsiness was underestimated among car drivers. Recent naturalistic driving studies show that, more than 50% of the time, drivers are doing *something* else while driving. The primary reason for underestimation from prior data is that it is nearly impossible to accurately determine the presence of distraction based on police crash investigations. After a crash, drivers can be dead, injured, dazed, may not remember what happened, or may be lying about what actually happened. What percentage of drivers who are involved in a crash while using their smartphones will admit doing so to an investigating officer? I would guess that it's probably less than 50% who are willing to self-report such behavior.

With the advent of naturalistic studies, researchers were able to actually view for the first time what drivers were doing during the seconds leading up to a crash or near-crash. These studies also let us determine how drivers behave and perform when they are just driving. This information, collected using volunteers, allows us to estimate the risk involved in engaging in such secondary tasks as eating a burger, dialing a phone, reading the newspaper, or applying makeup while driving.

Eyes forward, hands on the wheel

All of the VTTI naturalistic studies, as well as similar studies conducted by such colleagues as Jim Sayer at the University of Michigan, clearly show a recurring theme. The greatest distraction-related crash risks occur when the driver's eyes are away from the forward road, for whatever reason, in conjunction with an unexpected event happening simultaneously. In other words, a crash is imminent if these key ingredients are present to make our figurative cake. If I could give you one piece of general advice about driving safety, it would be to **KEEP YOUR EYES ON THE FORWARD ROAD**!

Visual distraction has been around for a long time. For many years, the classic example was manually tuning a radio. Most of us with a good bit of mileage probably know someone who had a crash or near-crash while tuning a radio, inserting a cassette or CD, or plugging in/changing the music on an iPod. I know a few.

The most interesting was my good friend, Bob, who was traveling an unfamiliar road at night in his VW Beetle. While looking down to find a good radio station, Bob missed a sharp turn. His Beetle launched itself onto a large shrub, with all four wheels off of the ground. If that wasn't bad enough, when Bob landed on the shrub, the muffler of his VW got knocked off, and his hand knocked the blaring aftermarket radio out of the dash and into the trunk (the engine was in back). Unfortunately, the radio wasn't wired through the ignition, and the car was high enough off of the ground to where Bob couldn't get into the trunk to turn down the radio. This made it difficult to go unnoticed, even in a very rural location. Bob eventually got the radio off and got a ride home, only to have a visit from the local sheriff the next morning.

My friend and colleague, Greg Fitch, has performed several impactful studies that highlight the issues of visual distraction while driving. Visual distraction has become a greater concern due to the advent of wireless devices like smartphones. The fact that smartphones are even called phones anymore is really a misnomer; you can do so many very distracting things with them outside of just making a call.

Regardless of what you are doing, you need to focus on keeping your eyes on the road. Specifically:

You need to develop an alarm in your head that tells you to look back at the road within two seconds, no matter what you are doing. If you do this, you will *halve* your crash risk relative to if you were to let yourself glance away from the road for more than two seconds.

The graph below illustrates this point.

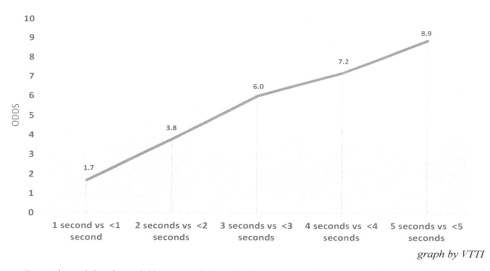

graph by VTTI

Practice this tip while you drive. When you choose to do something outside of the main driving task at hand, count "thousand one, thousand two" and see if your eyes are back on the road. Do the same when you are riding with others, especially younger drivers, and provide them with this sage advice. Even though your advanced knowledge of driving safety may seem unappreciated at the time, those you tell will at least think about this two-second alarm and may even begin to do it.

You also need to avoid looking away from the road more than a few times while performing a single non-driving task. This is another dimension to the "eyes-off-the-road" rule that you need to think about: The number of times you look away from the road, even when you are looking away for short periods of time because you've developed a trustworthy two-second alarm in your head.

Even with short glances away from the road, your awareness of your surroundings decreases. The probability of a crash occurring due to an unexpected event increases with each glance away from the road. The work conducted at VTTI continuously proves the point that:

Taking your eyes off of the road for more than six seconds, even in multiple short glances, begins to significantly increase your crash risk.

If you follow the two-second alarm advice, this means taking three glances away from the forward roadway. I would say this is the *maximum* amount of time you should take your eyes away from the road, but such time also depends greatly on where you are driving. If you are on a rural interstate in Kansas on a sunny, dry day with no other traffic around, you are probably okay taking a few short glances that total 10 or 12 seconds. If you are on the Washington, D.C., beltway in heavy traffic during a torrential rain storm, just wait until you are stopped or are safely at home before you perform any secondary task that takes your eyes off of the road *at all*. (Remember: ADAPT!)

With all of this information in mind, the following numbers provide some "best-guess" crash risk estimates for common secondary (that is, distracting) tasks performed while driving. The data are based on the VTTI naturalistic driving studies I mentioned above.

I am sure these numbers will change to some extent as we get more data. However, I also believe that these approximations won't change much in general, and I don't think that the factors shown as being the most or least risky will change at all.

Best-guess odds of crashing while "doing other stuff" at the same time

	Adult	Distracted Teen vs. Attentive Teen	Distracted Teen vs. Attentive Adult
Cell texting	5.0	6.0	10.0
Cell dialing	5.0	5.0	6.0
Cell reaching	4.0	6.0	8.0
Cell browsing	3.5	4.5	5.5
Cell talking	1.5	2.0	2.5
Vehicle (radio, A/C, etc.)	1.5	2.5	3.0
Reading (paper map, other)	10.0	8.0	12.0
Applying makeup	2.0	4.0	6.0
Eating	1.5	3.0	4.0
Drinking (non-alcohol)	1.3	2.5	3.0
Actively talking to passenger	1.2	2.0	2.5
Looking at outside object, person, etc.	5.0	8.0	12.0
Dispatching device (commercial drivers only)	10.0	N/A	N/A

There are several points to notice here:

1. You can't drive if you aren't looking at the road.

   Visual tasks that may also require a manual component have the highest crash risk. This means dialing, texting, reaching for a phone or any other object, or reading. There are many other possibilities, but KEEP YOUR EYES ON THE ROAD!

2. Teens are susceptible to more types of distractions than adults.

    As shown in the odds, eating, drinking, interacting with passengers, and vehicle operations appear to be somewhat higher-risk scenarios for teens when compared to adults. This is probably because the driving task itself requires more attention since teens are new at it. Thus, teens may get sucked in to the secondary tasks more and tend to forget about the primary task (*driving!*) a little more. I included the comparison to adults even though I need to remind everyone that teens start out with a crash rate that is three times higher than adults. This further highlights how risky secondary tasks are for teens.

3. You don't see nearly as large of an effect, for any of the drivers, for those tasks that require few, if any, glances away from the road. Which brings us to our next topic…

What about my talking car and my talking phone?

As a driver, you can now perform numerous tasks "hands-free" via Bluetooth and/or built-in systems. The most popular task is probably navigation, but you can also manipulate the temperature, radio, messaging, etc. of the vehicle via voice-only interactions.

Of course, a critical component of a well-designed hands-free system is that it also uses voice instead of a visual display to communicate information back to you. Again, looking at the road is critical in this situation. Anything you can do to keep your eyes on the road more while driving will reduce your crash risk. A key aspect to remember here is that you need a *well-designed* system.

There are plenty of studies that show no benefit to using a poorly designed hands-free operation when compared to performing the same task manually and visually. An example is a study conducted at VTTI in the late 1990s by a former student, Andy Gellatly. The study was designed to assess an earlier version of voice dialing. The system was inaccurate to the point where the driver had to look at the dashboard after every number to see if the system input the number correctly. If the number was wrong, the driver had to manually correct it. During the same study, we also found that voice commands made by the driver to this system were worse than looking down and manually dialing because the voice command actually took drivers' eyes off of the road more so than the visual dialing task!

So, use *well-designed* wireless systems when you can while driving, thus keeping your eyes on the road more.

Wait, Where Am I?

Mind wandering, lost in thought, or thinking about something else. These events are what we call *cognitive distraction* because your eyes are still presumably on the road but your mind is elsewhere. Many of us spend a lot of time in a car. And, let's face it, driving is often mundane. So, we do many things to keep our minds occupied. We make phone calls; truckers use CB radios; we listen to audio-books, music, news, conversations, podcasts. In fact:

More than 50% of the time, drivers are doing *something* in addition to driving. Just prior to crashes, drivers are doing something in addition to driving *almost 70% of the time.*

It was assumed for many years (and still is by some) that cognitive distraction:

1. Is a serious issue in driving that increases crash risk substantially.

2. Is something we can address.

At VTTI, we analyze a lot of real-world video of people crashing. The video comes from our naturalistic driving studies. As discussed several other times throughout this book, we have captured more than 1,500 crashes so far (we're still analyzing data as of this writing) with multi-camera systems that normally involve four to five cameras. In general, we rarely see a case during which someone is looking directly at something and runs into it. By contrast, we have seen several hundreds of cases during which a driver looks away at an inopportune time and crashes. This indicates that cognitive distraction is less risky than when a driver's eyes are off of the road, at least in relative terms. However, as I mentioned, we have seen those rare cases during which someone is clearly daydreaming or lost in thought and misses a traffic signal, stop sign, or other important sign. These cases do lead to crashes, sometimes very serious crashes. Therefore, the issue of cognitive distraction is important to discuss.

Cognitive distraction is a safety issue in driving, although much less so than visual distraction or fatigue. For instance, talking on a cell phone is considered a form of cognitive distraction because your eyes are on the road as opposed to, say, texting. The odds for talking on a cell phone are:

About 1.5 or so (odds = 1.5) if you are an adult, depending on the type of conversation. That risk increases for novice drivers to about 2.5 (odds = 2.5). Texting on a phone, however, increases crash risk *between 4.0 and 23.0 times* (odds = 4.0 – 23.0), depending on vehicle type and driver.

An interesting study recently performed by our friends at the Insurance Institute for Highway Safety (IIHS) used the VTTI 100-Car Naturalistic Driving Study data to determine that engaging in cell conversations while driving does not significantly increase crash risk. The IIHS made this statement because drivers often cognitively disengage from driving by doing *something*, even if they aren't involved in a cell phone conversation.

It has become popular to debate the risk of a cell conversation while driving as a main type of cognitive distraction. However, I believe that there may be just as much increase in risk while listening to a good audiobook or podcast. There are advocates you may hear in the news who will say otherwise. They will argue that a cell phone conversation can be more "emotional" or that the driver is compelled to keep the phone conversation going even when driving demands 100% attention because the other person is not in the driving "context," and to interrupt the conversation seems "rude" to the driver.

Despite its relatively small increase in risk, cognitive distraction is something to which we should pay attention (pun intended) and try to do something about. That is, any risk increase is not good because our ultimate goal here is to let you survive the drive. With that in mind, I have three pieces of advice to keep you safe and to minimize your risk of experiencing cognitive distraction:

1. Keep the primary task primary.

   I think one trap drivers fall into, particularly novice and/or young drivers, is forgetting which of the two (or three, or four) things they are doing is most important. Take, for example, a cell phone conversation. In terms of driving, keep the conversation where it belongs: As something that you do when the road, weather, and traffic allow it. In other words, a cell conversation should be the SECONDARY task while you prudently control your giant piece of metal hurtling down the roadway. If you feel yourself getting sucked into the conversation emotionally because your girlfriend is breaking up with you or your kid is flunking French, find a safe place to pull over and continue the call.

2. Be rude!

   This is the one time you shouldn't listen to your mother. It can never be emphasized enough: Your primary task is to drive. Talking is a secondary task that should only be engaged in while driving under ideal conditions when traffic is light and weather conditions permit. If such conditions change, interrupt the cell conversation, and tell mom, dad, or junior that you'll call back later.

3. Hang up, turn off the stereo, put down the cheese fries, and adapt to survive.

That's right, turn off the music, as much as it pains me to write that. If situations in the driving environment become bad or difficult, you need to focus your attention on the driving task, not continue to figure out the lyrics to your favorite Natural Child song.

Impairment Not

Why don't you talk about this TV in my car with a map on it?

At this point, you may be asking yourself "What's wrong with this guy? I have this TV in the dash of my new Tesla with a map on it, and he's not even talking about how distracting it is?" To which I say, yes, but have you considered that navigating to a destination is (presumably) not a secondary task because you need to know how to get there so you can, in fact, get there? When it comes to navigating, there is significant risk in the form of more road time (exposure), missed turns, and/or searching for signs when you are lost. Navigating is a necessary part of the driving task.

The dissertation for my Ph.D. in 1985 was the first on-road investigation of the safety associated with the use of an in-car navigation system. With the help of my advisor, Walt Wierwille, and my lab mates, Jon Antin and Melissa (now my wife), we designed an early prototype of an instrumented vehicle with cameras and other sensors that measured real-world driving performance. A photo is shown here of that first instrumentation, which became the basis for the VTTI naturalistic driving study research method. This

setup was beyond the state of the art in 1985, but it certainly looks less sophisticated than what we use today. In fact, we build systems now slightly larger than a box of playing cards that are much more capable than the one shown.

There are several stories associated with driving around this vehicle with cameras strapped all over it. Many drivers would politely honk at our volunteer subject because they thought he or she had inadvertently left something on the roof of the vehicle. Since we were doing a controlled navigation study, the destination was always the same: A little suburban neighborhood in Southwest Virginia. Unfortunately, the rumor started in this neighborhood that we were actually from the IRS and were taking pictures of people's houses to determine who would be subjected to a tax audit. After a few times of running this instrumented vehicle, the neighbors would call the police every time we stopped to switch drivers. It was a little unnerving to our test subjects to have to interact with the police, but hey, that's field research.

So, given that navigation was an essential part of the driving task, the question for this study then became: What is the best way to navigate while driving?

We found that, after performing the main study described above and several others, including a study in the mid-1990s I conducted with my friend and former student, Dan McGehee, using 100 vehicles in Orlando:

1. Moving maps that are *well-designed* are less visually demanding than paper maps or direction lists.

2. Turn-by-turn screens are less visually demanding than moving maps.

3. Adding *well-designed* voice commands to either moving maps or turn-by-turn screens reduced the visual demand placed on the driver.

4. If they work well, voice commands alone are the least visually demanding option.

Notice in the last result that I said voice commands alone are the least visually demanding, not the least distracting. This is because, again, navigation is part of the driving task. Essentially, if you have a good, *well-designed* voice navigation system, your risk is reduced compared to any other navigation option available.

Speaking of Attentive and Alert... A Few Tips for Commercial Drivers

When you write a book like this, it is sometimes hard to know when to call it good. In addition to motorcycles, which are covered later, I struggled with what to say about long-haul or line-haul (that is, BIG) trucks. I opted not to include heavy trucks from the trucker's viewpoint, primarily because it would be its own book. This is because truck driving is MUCH different than "four-wheel" driving. Truck drivers have special training; special licenses, such as the commercial driver's license; special regulations that include hours of service; differing laws, such as zero tolerance for alcohol; different medical requirements; and a different lifestyle that leads to sleep- and health-related issues, among others. Someday, I may work with my truck and bus colleagues to write a book about heavy trucks, if this book does okay.

Although we all think of the long-haul, big semi-tractor trailers when we first think of trucks, they actually constitute only about 10% of the trucks on the road today. There are many other commercial trucks that make shorter deliveries. These local/short-haul trucks do not have to adhere to many of the same requirements as interstate trucks. In addition, there are many, many people in the U.S. and around the world who drive something other than trucks for a living, including taxis and limousines.

If you are in this group, congratulations! You have one of the most dangerous occupations in the United States! If you are a farmer/rancher, logger, or construction worker and you say "No way," I have news for you. Many risks occur while in, or driving, a vehicle. In fact, professional drivers rival commercial fishing for the top spot of the most dangerous occupation in some cases.

A big reason for your on-the-job risk as a professional driver is your *exposure*. If you have read to this point, you have seen the phrases "crash *rate*" or "fatal crash *rate*" several times. The rate is typically per mile traveled; even when the rate is low, your risk still increases with every mile you drive. And many of you professional drivers cover a lot of miles. This makes a lot of the advice in this book even more important for you. Since your exposure is necessarily very high due to your job, lowering your risk per mile traveled is critical.

So, here are just a couple of tips that I have for y'all:

1. Many of you get paid by the mile or trip, but don't let the money or job pressure make you lose sight of the consequences of your actions while driving.

    Some of you carry perishable goods that need to be delivered in a shorter timeframe than other types of cargo. Some of you are supposed to make a very large number of sales calls every day, which means you are more or less expected to work while you drive. Still others of you have to meet some arbitrary deadline, such as "Will be delivered in 30 minutes or less, or your pizza is free…" Many of you get paid more money if you can make more trips in the same amount of time.

2. These rules incentivize professional drivers to drive while distracted, drive even when drowsy, drive as fast as possible, and/or drive aggressively. As a professional driver, you need to try and avoid these traps, for your own safety and the safety of others. Be wary of these tendencies, because they can sneak up on you!

3. Even though you have a high level of practice and skill, you still have to look at the road.

I have been involved in a number of legal cases and given congressional testimony about driving distraction. I have heard arguments that commercial drivers are professional and are highly skilled, or that they are trained enough so that they can drive while doing other things like reading, writing, or interacting with dispatching devices. Rich Hanowski and his colleagues in the VTTI Center for Truck and Bus Safety did a distraction study during which they estimated crash and near-crash risks when drivers performed a variety of tasks. Next to cell phone texting, they found interacting with electronic dispatching devices to be the most risky for commercial drivers. In fact:

When a commercial driver is using a dispatching device, he or she is at *10 times greater risk* (odds = 10.0) than when just driving.

Many of you need to use such devices while driving to get your next load or fare, and I get that. But some of these devices are very badly designed and require you to take your eyes off of the road for too long. Try to find ways to do what you need to do with as few short glances (remember, less than two seconds) away from the road as possible. If the message on your dispatching device is long or you have to type, you really need to pull over in a safe spot to read and/or type!

4. The moral here is that, no matter how much experience or skill you have, you can't drive safely when you are looking away from the road a lot or for long periods.

    Take a look at this chapter for more details about what is and isn't okay when it comes to driving distraction; the risks outlined there apply to you professional drivers, too.

5. Fatigue is an even more serious issue for some professional drivers.

    Most of you aren't regulated for hours of service, and many of you work long shifts. This puts you at greater risk for drowsiness than private vehicle drivers. As I mentioned earlier in this chapter, if you are tired enough to experience slow eyelid closures or head bobbing, you just have to take a break and, preferably, a nap.

General Resources

http://www.ncbi.nlm.nih.gov/pmc/articles/PMC4001675/

http://www.distraction.gov/downloads/pdfs/the-impact-of-hand-held-and-hands-free-cell-phone-use-on-driving-performance-and-safety-critical-event-risk.pdf

http://www.distraction.gov/downloads/pdfs/driver-distraction-commercial-vehicle-operations.pdf

http://www.apps.vtti.vt.edu/PDFs/ndrs-2014/Simons-Morton-2014.pdf

http://www.iihs.org/iihs/sr/statusreport/article/49/8/1

Klauer, S. G., Guo, F., Simons-Morton, B., Ouimet, M.C., Lee, S.E., & Dingus T. A. (2014). Distracted Driving and Risk of Road Crashes among Novice and Experienced Drivers. *New England Journal of Medicine, 370*, 54-59.

Sayer, J., Devonshire, J.M., & Flannagan, C. (2005). *The effects of secondary task performance on naturalistic driving* (Technical report No. UMTRI-2005-29).

Neale, V. L., Dingus, T. A., Garness, S. A., Keisler, A. S., & Carroll, R. J. (2002). The relationship between truck driver sleeper berth sleep quality and safety-related critical events. In *Proceedings of the Third International Truck and Bus Safety Research and Policy Symposium*, 65-78.

Dingus, T. A., Hardee, H. L., & Wierwille, W. W. (1987). Development of models for on-board detection of driver impairment. *Accident Analysis & Prevention, 19*(4), 271-283. doi:10.1016/0001-4575(87)90062-5

Dingus, T. A., Antin, J. F., Hulse, M. C., & Wierwille, W. W. (1986). *Human Factors Test and Evaluation of an Automobile Moving-Map Navigation System Part I: Attentional Demand Requirements.* Warren, MI: General Motors Research Laboratories.

Blanco, M., Bocanegra, J.L., Morgan, J.F., Fitch, G.M., Medina, A., Olson, R.L., Hanowski, R.J., Daily, B., & Zimmermann, R.P. (2009). *Assessment of a Drowsy Driver Warning System for Heavy Vehicle Drivers: Final Report* (Report No. DOT HS 811 117). Washington, DC: National Highway Traffic Safety Administration.

Gellatly, A. W., & Dingus, T. A. (1998). Speech recognition and automotive applications: using speech to perform in-vehicle tasks. In *Proceedings of the Human Factors and Ergonomics Society Annual Meeting, 42*(17), 1247-1251. doi:10.1177/154193129804201715

Dingus, T. A., Hulse, M. C., McGehee, D. V., Manakkal, R., & Fleischman, R. N. (1994). Driver performance results from the TravTek IVHS camera car evaluation study. In *Proceedings of the Human Factors and Ergonomics Society Annual Meeting, 38*(17), 1118-1122. doi:10.1177/154193129403801710

Chapter 7.

Be Kind and Caring

It's not just you on the road. It's you, plus 210 million other licensed drivers in the U.S. alone (and, let's face it, quite a few unlicensed drivers), plus bicyclists, plus motorcyclists, plus tractor trailers…

This chapter provides information about how to more peacefully and safely travel among your fellow transportation users.

Aggressive Driving 101

Make love, not war

Would you pull a gun on another driver who annoyed you? If so, just stop reading, seek anger management counseling, and/or turn yourself in. If not, are you really willing to use your car as a weapon? Because what you're driving is a couple of tons of steel traveling at a high rate of speed that can be just as deadly as any weapon.

This may seem like an extreme statement, but aggressive driving is a real issue. We have all seen cases during which folks tailgate at 70 mph and/or weave in and out of traffic with very close spacing. Yes, most such offenders are men, and yes, most of them are younger men, which reiterates my point in Chapter 5 about testosterone.

Our friends at the AAA Foundation for Traffic Safety estimate that:

More than half of fatal crashes involve aggressive driving.

That's a significant number. It's important to note that this statistic includes excessive speeding, which accounts for about two-thirds of the total aggressive driving risk in the AAA definition. A lot of people are killed because someone is in too much of a hurry to function safely within traffic and road conditions.

Related to this behavior is an interesting study done in the late 1990s. My colleagues, Bob Ervin and Paul Fancher, now both retired, did an early study at the University of Michigan about adaptive cruise control. Adaptive cruise control allows you to set your following distance, not just your following speed as is the case in regular cruise control. Adaptive cruise control uses radar to set your "headway" to the vehicle in front, keeping you at a constant distance until you have clear space in front of you, at which point the vehicle returns to the set speed, just like cruise control. Using the data generated from this radar, our Michigan friends were able to determine much about following behavior.

They found that there are basically two kinds of drivers: "Hunters" and "gliders." Hunters are always pushing the system some, trying to find a quicker way forward. Gliders are just generally happy to go with the flow of traffic. I am a hunter, but I wish I was a glider. Family and friends who are gliders really get to the destination almost as fast as I do, and with much less stress. Of course, an extreme case of being a hunter is being an overly aggressive driver and putting yourself and others in danger. Here is a classic example of this type of behavior: A male driver (because it is almost always a male behaving this way) is traveling a divided four-lane highway, with both lanes pretty full of cars. The driver is weaving in and out of traffic at very close spacing to get to wherever he is headed. However, he only arrives 15 seconds earlier because there was no way to make any real difference in time due to the traffic volume. Other dangerous cases of aggressive driving include passing a bicycle at a close distance or passing a car on a two-way road with too short of a sight distance.

Bill Murray summed it up best to his truck-wielding groundhog companion in *Groundhog Day*: "Don't drive angry. Don't drive angry!" And Bill was right. Recent research shows that driving angry or in some other elevated emotional state:

Increases your crash risk by 10 times (odds ratio = 10.0) compared to normal driving.

Like it or not, driving is a social endeavor

If you are a hunter, we all understand. However, you should know when to chill out. Know when to not get too aggressive and risk putting us all in danger. Learn what it took me 25 years to learn: All of your efforts to get ahead in traffic don't really speed things up that much. That doesn't mean you can't look ahead, plan ahead, and *be efficient* as you travel, which are all good ideas for a number of reasons described in this book. It really just means don't engage in extreme driving behavior.

If you are a glider, don't be the cause of aggressive driving. There *are* hunters in the world, and you care less than they do, so get out of their way. The ultimate example here that drives all hunters crazy is the glider driver who has his or her cruise control set on 70.001 mph while in the left lane when the traffic in the right lane is going 70.000 mph. The left lane used to be, and still is in many other countries, the *fast* or *passing* lane. Hang out in the left lane in Germany and see what happens, for example. Don't drive in the left lane because you like it; don't stay there after you pass something; and, most of all, don't try to be socially conscious and slow others down. This type of behavior only leads to frustration and increased aggressive driving all around. Move into the left lane to pass, pass briskly (especially around trucks), and move back to the right lane once you have passed.

Another example of driving as a social endeavor relates to a small survey VTTI conducted about 10 years ago in the Washington, D.C., area. We asked people when and why they chose not to use turn signals. Roughly 57% of drivers did not use signals, at least part of the time. We found many reasons given for not using a turn signal, but the most interesting response was "If I signal, other drivers will close the gap I am trying to get into…" This is a form of aggressive driving behavior. In the long run, though, it's better to be polite. Let people go in front of you; merge out of a closed lane before you get to the end and avoid slowing everyone down; and, if someone uses his or her turn signal, make room for that driver and resist "closing the gap."

If you are often on the receiving end of a variety of pointed gestures from other drivers beyond a hand wave, you should look in the mirror, both the one at home and the rearview mirror in your car. Whether you are a hunter or a glider, you may want to think about how much a little courtesy is really costing you. I guarantee, it's not much.

My last little piece of socially conscious advice may save you in a more direct way: Dim your headlights at night when other cars are coming. It seems obvious, but I wish I had a dollar for each time I passed a car or truck with high beams on. If you've put a lift kit on your truck (I am from Southwest Virginia, after all), get your headlamps re-aimed. If you are carrying a load that moves your low beams too high, maybe just consider traveling in daylight.

Vulnerable Road Users

"Vulnerable road users" is a term generally used at VTTI and elsewhere to describe those who are essentially unprotected by steel, shatterproof glass, airbags, and crumple zones. It's a relatively self-explanatory term: Such users are more susceptible to injuries and fatalities. During recent years, the numbers of fatalities for vulnerable road users have generally plateaued or increased while car fatalities have decreased. Most pedestrian and bicycle fatalities are male (69% and 88%, respectively), and most occur in urban areas (73% and 69%, respectively). Conspicuity, which is how well the vulnerable road user can be seen, and alcohol are the major factors at play when it comes to vulnerable road user risk.

One certain way to reduce crashes and fatalities is to separate the vulnerable from the non-vulnerable users. Sidewalks, bike trails, and bike lanes are always going to help reduce fatalities. However, if you have to share the road, here are a few tips:

For the non-vulnerable users

1. Have a good mental model of the kind of vulnerable user with whom you are interacting.

   I think numerous conflicts and crashes occur because the car driver is treating the vulnerable user like the wrong type of vehicle. Here is how I tend to classify vulnerable road users:

   Bicycle = Runner
   Electric bicycle = Bicycle
   Scooter = Bicycle
   Motorcycle or big scooter = Car

   The key questions to ask when making such a classification are: Do such drivers occupy and have the right to an entire vehicle travel lane? Or do you treat them as being on the side of the road, passing when it is safe? In either case, you want to give a wide berth if and when you choose to pass. But how and when you safely pass is dictated by the above logic.

2. Be mellow; you don't have X-ray vision.

   Talking to bicycle enthusiasts, this is probably the complaint I hear most about their four-wheel friends: Those of the four-wheel variety tend to pass bicyclists when there is no way they can see far enough ahead, often cutting too close or cutting off bicyclists. The key here is to be patient.

For the vulnerable users

1. Obey the rules of the road.

    Don't violate the expectations of those who could run over you!
    No matter your mode of transport, follow the rules of the road.
    There are numerous intersection fatalities, for example, so make
    sure you don't violate signals or run stop signs.

2. Be conspicuous!

    Wear reflective and or bright-/light-colored clothing. Make sure
    you have a lot of reflectors on your backpack or bike. Use lights
    and flashing lights on your bike. In general, assume drivers don't
    see you, because often they don't!

from the author's personal photo collection

General Resources

https://www.aaafoundation.org/aggressive-driving

http://www.pedbikeinfo.org/data/factsheet_crash.cfm

Fancher, P., Ervin, R., & Bogard, S. (1998). *A Field Operational Test of Adaptive Cruise Control System Operability in Naturalistic Use* (SAE Technical Paper No. 980852). doi:10.4271/980852

Fancher, P., Ervin, R., Sayer, J., Hagan, M., Bogard, S., Bareket, Z., Mefford, M., & Haugen, J. (1997). *Intelligent Cruise Control Field Operational Test* (Interim Report No. UMTRI-97-11). Ann Arbor, Michigan: The University of Michigan Transportation Research Institute.

Chapter 8.

Be a Helicopter Parent . . . for This! (If You Are a Teen, Enjoy the Breeze!)

Newly licensed teen drivers are *three times more likely* to get into a fatal crash than their adult counterparts.

That is a huge, scary, and very sad statistic. In fact, teens are more likely to die in a car crash than they are to die due to ALL other sources of unintentional injury and disease COMBINED. There are few teens these days who have not been touched by a crash, either directly or indirectly. Most know a friend, acquaintance, or class-mate who has been killed in a car wreck. If you are a teen driver, pay attention to this book. If you are a parent/guardian of a teen driver, pay even closer attention, because this is reality.

When it comes to driving, your life can change completely (or end) *in one second*. Leave Tokyo drifting for the movies and *Grand Theft Auto* for the basement.

A friend and colleague, Bruce Simons-Morton, has been studying teens and health for many years while working for the National In-stitutes of Health. About 10 years ago, I met Bruce because he real-ized that the biggest risk to teens is driving and that he needed more data about the topic. I knew that VTTI needed to focus more of its work on the riskiest driving group: Newly licensed teens. Bruce and I have now performed several naturalistic driving studies together with our VTTI and National Institutes of Health colleagues. Along the way, we have discovered a number of interesting findings about teen drivers.

One of the most important discoveries made is that most teens essentially know how to handle a vehicle and know how to drive safely; *they just often choose not to drive safely*. This is important because it sheds light on the debate about whether teens need more or better driver education/training or whether teens need more supervision, age, and maturity relative to driving. More and better training will always be important, but the critical issue relative to teen driving risk appears to be the latter.

Two examples illustrate this point. With sponsorship from the National Institutes of Health, VTTI did a naturalistic driving study during which we instrumented the cars of 42 newly licensed teens (they all volunteered for the study) for 18 months with unobtrusive cameras and sensors. One of the analyses we performed sought to characterize errors that teens make while merging in traffic. In general, we found that teens make the same number as or fewer errors than adults. In other words, teens know and follow the rules, such as using turn signals, matching speed, and checking blind spots, at least as well as adults. Therefore, teens know how to successfully complete this complex maneuver.

The second example is illustrated in the figure below. We measured many factors about what teens do when they drive, including braking hard, swerving, speeding, and "hitting the gas." We call these collective factors risky vehicle-based driving behaviors. The higher the rate of these risky driving behaviors, the greater the likelihood of a crash. As shown, adults in our study engaged in these behaviors *about four to five times less frequently* than the teens…except when teens had an adult in the car, during which time teens exhibited risky driving behaviors *at about the same rate as the adults.*

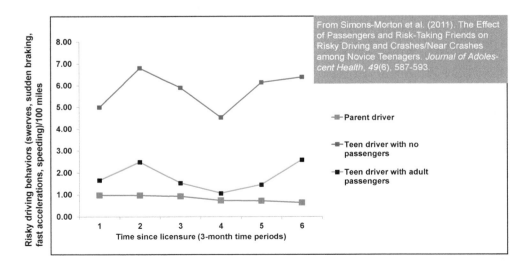

From Simons-Morton et al. (2011). The Effect of Passengers and Risk-Taking Friends on Risky Driving and Crashes/Near Crashes among Novice Teenagers. *Journal of Adolescent Health, 49*(6), 587-593.

This finding was consistent for other types of risky driving behaviors, such as driving while distracted. In other words, the teens drove like adults when they were supervised, but they drove like a creature from another planet when adults were not present. This led us to the conclusion that (and I know I am being repetitive here, but we're big on redundancy in our line of work):

Most teen drivers pretty much know how to drive safely, they just choose not to.

How do you as a parent or guardian of a teen driver ensure your teen's overall safety while on the road? Just keep reading...

photo courtesy of VTTI

When I Was Your Age, I Drove that Old '85 Gremlin...

Much like the car you select for yourself, the car you choose for your teen can make a significant difference when it comes to the risk of getting into a fatal crash. Essentially, you are looking for the crash-worthiness of a vehicle. If families were to put their teen drivers in the newest car they owned instead of the oldest, it is estimated that:

The teen fatality rate would *drop by one-third nationwide.*

Our friends at the Insurance Institute for Highway Safety (IIHS) provide advice about cars that are good for your teen to drive. In general, these cars are newer, have multiple safety features, and are at least moderate in size and weight (vehicle mass being an important factor in mitigating crash risk). So, assuming you have selected the best car you can afford to own for your teen, what's next?

Training Your Teen to Drive

If you are a novice at anything, you will make lots of mistakes. This is true of everything, from basketball to chess to driving. Unfortunately, mistakes in driving can have very high consequences. With driving, crash rates are the highest when you first get your license, regardless of your age. However, the younger the driver, the higher the crash rate. The good news is that the risks for young novice drivers decline rapidly after the first six months of licensure. However, their risk does not reach the low crash rates of experienced adults for about six years!

I have to say that training my two kids to drive and then letting them go once they were licensed marked two of my most harrowing parental experiences. Of course, it's easy to argue that I was anxious because of what I've seen in my profession. After all, I spend all day reading about crashes and such. That may be a correct assumption, but only because I was fully aware of the risks my kids could and would face on the road. But congratulations! Now that you are reading this, we will be in the same boat! Feel free to call your friends with kids at 2 a.m. on prom night; they will be up to console you.

There are multiple articles and opinions about training teens to drive. Advice abounds about the "correct" way to teach teens to drive, from the old-fashioned way of riding around with parents for a while to attending very expensive driving and even racing schools. Frankly, the results of these schools of thought are pretty mixed. Assuming that the teen spends enough time behind the wheel, all of these methods generally teach teen drivers the fundamentals of how to control a car and interact with traffic. The driver's test requirement ensures teens can drive at a basic level and understand the rules of the road, for the most part. However, teen drivers not knowing what to do and how to do it are not the greatest issues when it comes to risk; ultimately, it is their *choosing not to* that I believe is the biggest safety issue. So, here are a few tips for effectively training your teens to drive:

1. Emphasize your expectation for safe, attentive, low-risk driving.

   It is necessary to teach your teens vehicle management skills like steering, braking, and the rules of the road. Even more importantly, you need to emphasize no speeding, no distractions, no alcohol, and no aggressive driving.

2. Teens don't recognize hazardous situations very well.

   A friend and colleague, Don Fisher, from the University of Massachusetts, has conducted significant research into this very topic. It is important to teach your kids to always anticipate and understand what *might happen* while driving. A car or a pedestrian may unexpectedly pop out from behind a service vehicle or a parked delivery truck. A driver making a left turn in front of you might assume you are going to stop at a yellow light. Heavy traffic on the interstate might suddenly slow to a stop because of congestion. You get the picture.

   As you drive around with your teen(s), try to point out these types of surprising events. Don't assume that they see what you see. When they start to complain because you are being redundant and claim that what you are saying is obvious, you should *start* to feel good about teaching them effective driving behaviors.

3. Teach your teen(s) to see, not just look.

    My experiences with both of my kids led me to understand that they would dutifully pull up to a stop sign, look twice both ways, and sometimes pull out in front of a car anyway. Teens don't always fully grasp the concept of sight distance. Not only do they need to be able to see, they need to be able to see far enough, even if they have to creep ahead at the intersection, wait a while to pass a bicycle, or look farther around the curve.

4. Don't just look; look ahead.

    In general, you should teach your teen(s) to look as far down the road as they can reasonably do and to anticipate what is occurring ahead, in addition to simply keeping the car in the lane. There is nothing handier than seeing the brake lights of a vehicle two cars ahead or the slow-moving truck while you can comfortably change lanes to pass.

5. Drive around, a lot.

    Studies show that the more supervised driving hours teens receive, the better off they are when they become independent drivers. Even though you may be like me wherein 45 hours of driving with my kids seemed like 450, do as much supervised driving with your teen as you can. Benefits have been shown with up to 70 hours of supervised driving.

6. Put your teen driver(s) in unusual situations.

    As is true with many new drivers, teens typically handle vehicles well until they are faced with a situation they have never experienced. So, when it snows, take your teen(s) to the empty shopping center and have them spin out and correct the vehicle. If it's icy, make them practice going slow and steering and stopping in full control; also make them stop while going downhill (at a safe location so you're not endangering other drivers while practicing). Have your teen drive in the fog and point out that they can't see far enough ahead to stop. Take them as a passenger to a pedestrian area on a Saturday night (college towns are good for this scenario), and let them watch the kids pop out from between cars. Let them drive (for a while; watch for drowsiness symptoms!) on a long trip so they understand what it's like to get tired while driving.

There are multiple unusual scenarios you could teach. Try to give your teen the broadest range of driving experiences that you can. As I discussed earlier, my daughter would have benefited from a good hydroplaning lesson.

7. Forget racing school.

If they want, your kids can pay for this themselves when they are adults. There are numerous performance racing-type schools, and they all claim great benefits when it comes to teaching driving skills. Such programs are expensive, and it has become somewhat popular amongst those who can afford it to send their teens to one. I do believe that racing schools can teach a higher level of driving skills while making teens more confident in their driving abilities. But therein lies the problem: Regardless of the skills acquired, an overconfident teen driver is a dangerous thing behind the wheel of a car.

8. Be calm, patient, and constructive.

Staying calm and patient while teaching my kids to drive was, by far, the hardest part for me. It's difficult to remain calm when your kid is about to hit something. At VTTI, my friend, former student, and colleague, Charlie Klauer, and our friends at the National Institutes of Health are currently conducting a teen practice driving study. While the results are just beginning to come in as of this writing, one thing is abundantly clear: There are large differences in outcomes based on the skill and patience of parents or guardians trying to teach their teens to drive.

The most successful parents or guardians give constructive advice, use mistakes as a teachable moment to illustrate more general concepts, and are patient and calm even when their teens are not. I know it's easier to say than to actually do this, but it's important to remain at ease and under control when teaching a teen driver.

The rules of the road are one thing; the rules of "the house" are equally important

When I was 15 and living in Rochester, Minnesota, my family lived a couple of miles from the local drive-in theater. That summer, I was allowed to take the family car to see the movies with my friends. What I remember most about that period was "buck night" on Wednesdays, when it cost one dollar for a carload to get into the drive-in. What do you think we did? Of course we piled a dozen kids into my mother's Mercury Monterey—in both the passenger compartment and the trunk—and cruised over to the movies. Sometimes, friends managed to get some beers.

An interesting related fact you should know is that I didn't have a driver's license or even a permit at that time. While my parents (mostly my father) had good intentions by loaning me the family vehicle, this was a recipe for disaster: An overloaded car, no seat belts, under-aged kids, lots of testosterone, and novice alcohol use. My dad's logic was, I suppose, that the drive-in was so close to home that nothing truly bad could happen during such a short trip on what was a lightly traveled rural road. My father was, of course, assuming that we wouldn't drive somewhere else. In this case, the rules of the house when it came to driving were much too trusting and, thus, very dangerous. In hindsight, this may be why my acute interest in risk management developed: Out of a survival instinct.

A fundamental question every parent or guardian needs to answer is: Do you believe driving is a right or a privilege? If you are a teen about to start driving, I know what you are going to say. However, your parents will probably disagree with you. After all, they likely bought the car, pay for the insurance, and are taking a chance that you will keep it together in a dangerous endeavor.

The point is, parents or guardians deserve the right to make and enforce the "house" rules with respect to teen driving. It is both common and beneficial these days for parents or guardians to enter into a contract with their teen driver(s) outlining the rules and the consequences of violating those rules. It is imperative that both parties agree to such a contract.

One form of a teen driving contract goes beyond a basic agreement and has been shown to be of benefit. This type of contract is known as "checkpoints." Checkpoints have to do with earning additional independence while driving when certain milestones are reached in good standing. This is based upon a concept called "graduated driver's licensing," or GDL. All states have different GDL laws with respect to newly permitted and licensed drivers. The most accurate statements I can make about these GDL rules are that the stronger rules save a lot of lives and the rules of each state are all over the map (pun intended).

Our friends at the IIHS have developed a handy tool that shows the GDL laws by state and how your teen's crash risk would be lowered if *you* (or your state) enacted more stringent GDL rules. Research has shown that an ideal set of GDL rules includes:

1. Issuing a driver's permit on the teen's 16th birthday;

2. Receiving 70 hours of supervised practice driving;

3. Issuing the driver's license on the teen's 17th birthday;

4. No unsupervised nighttime driving occurring after 8 p.m.; and

5. No teen passengers without supervision until the teen driver is 18 years of age.

Depending on the state, the fatal crash risk for your teen could be *reduced by more than 50%* by imposing such a strict set of rules as part of a checkpoint program.

If broken down by individual states, South Dakota would receive the greatest benefit of implementing all of the rules, with a 63% reduction in fatal crashes.

There are clearly tremendous benefits to enacting such rules in a checkpoint manner. The most important factor at play is keeping teen drivers safe and alive. I raised two teens, and I know that telling your kids they can't drive unless they follow these rules isn't going to be a pleasant conversation, particularly if their friends don't have to follow the same rules. While some aspects of the ideal rules may be difficult or even impractical for many families to implement, at least consider enacting some or all of them to some extent. The aforementioned IIHS calculator lets you input different levels of different rules to gauge your teen's crash risk, such as no nighttime driving after 10 p.m. instead of 8 p.m. or having one teen passenger present instead of none. I strongly recommend that you work out a set of rules that keeps your teens as safe as possible while being (mostly) agreeable to all involved. Be strong, and know that your teen will love you again when he or she is 25!

Teens and Alcohol

A few years ago, VTTI was visited by some German colleagues. We presented some of our research that was of mutual interest, including our teen driving research. The young driver fatality rate is much lower in Germany than it is in the U.S., thanks in no small part to the minimum driving age (18 years of age). However, the interesting part of the conversation was that our German colleagues felt strongly that we had things backwards with respect to alcohol and driving. Their opinion was that, since the drinking age in Germany is 16 and the driving age is 18, German teens have two years to get used to the effects of alcohol and two years for the novelty of drinking alcohol to wear off before they are able to get behind the wheel.

While this may be true to some extent, there are other safety factors at play. For example, if you are stopped at a traffic stop in Germany or in a number of other countries, such as Australia, you breathe into the tube to check your blood alcohol content (BAC) or you lose your license for a very long time. If you breathe into the tube and are over the legal BAC limit (0.05% in Germany), you also lose your license for a very long time. No muss, no fuss, done deal. Therefore, people of all ages drink and drive less in Germany, and many other countries, than they do in the United States.

It is true that the U.S. has an issue with drinking and driving at all ages, even among ages 16 to 20 when there is *zero tolerance* for alcohol while driving a car. Some interesting statistics related to this point:

- 90% of college freshmen in the U.S. drink alcohol even though they are (almost) all breaking the law.

- 15% of 16- to 17-year-old drivers involved in a fatal crash had a BAC above the *adult* legal limit of 0.08%.

- 30% of 18- to 20-year-old drivers involved in a fatal crash had a BAC above the *adult* legal limit of 0.08%.

- About one-half of all fatalities and serious injuries due to alcohol-related crashes happen to passengers, so not riding with an intoxicated driver is just as important as not driving while intoxicated.

You should never assume that your teens won't drink and drive or that their friends won't be driving them around after drinking, even at age 16.

This next piece of advice is merely a personal opinion that I think is critically important. I know it won't sit well with everybody, though. I always told my kids that, if they decided to drink and drive or to drink and ride in a car with someone who has also been drinking, they wouldn't have to worry about a crash. Because I would kill them myself. Realistically, I knew they would probably find themselves in a situation during which they didn't have great options to make a good choice. So, I also told my kids and their friends that, if they needed a ride, at any time of the day or night, for whatever reason, I would pick them up. No questions asked. No punishment of any kind (unless you count my long, arduous lecturing as punishment). All they had to do was call and ask. During the time my kids were 16 to 22 years of age, I probably received 10 such calls from my two kids and one or two of their friends. It was well worth the sleep lost.

Interestingly enough, both my kids are very moderate drinkers the majority of the time. They both have pocket Breathalyzers. My daughter has a BAC calculator app on her smartphone. They take it very, very seriously. Just recently, they were both back in town (they are now 21 and 23) and were downtown with several of their friends. They all decided to celebrate a bit and take the local van ride service that generally charges $5 per person. This night, however, the driver wanted $150 for four of them (get it, holidays, freezing rain, bars closed, I can charge what I want…shame on you!). Anyway, I got "the call" and was very happy to get it. I was tired, it was late and cold out, but it was so much better to get that call than the other call all parents or guardians dread.

Teens and Sleep

Studies have shown that 16- to 18-year-olds need between 8.5 and 9.5 hours of sleep each night. Due to circadian rhythm effects, the ideal time for teens to awake is around 8 a.m. Of course, for a variety of reasons, teens have to get up earlier to make it to school in many places. Many teens, therefore, don't get enough sleep. Why am I telling you this? Because a recent University of Minnesota study showed that:

A later start time at school *reduced teen crashes by about 70%.*

Do what you can to make sure your teens are getting a reasonable amount of sleep, particularly if they have longer drives to school or work or have a long trip on the horizon.

Keep an Eye on Your Teens

The chart included in the first section of this chapter shows you a very scary occurrence: When there are no adults around, our teens often choose not to drive safely even though they know how.

In reality, some teens are very risky by nature, while some are not. But it's hard to know which is which. Risk taking is a very complex thing. We have all known teens who tend to be risky. However, there are cases when seemingly low-risk teens have episodes of risky behavior. I have heard numerous stories of the "model child" who had a beer or two at a party and crashed a vehicle going 90 mph, or texted while driving and crossed the center line, or missed a turn in their new sports car and rolled several times.

Some of you may remember the old Cold War strategy of "trust but verify," which is why we had treaties enacted while satellites watched our potential enemies. This approach can also be used in teen driving. Essentially, you are in a "Cold War" with your kids, even with a treaty in place, such as the driving contracts described earlier. Even if your teens have gained your trust after a lifetime of teaching them what's right and what's wrong, it is still important to get verification. One method of such verification is to form somewhat of a coalition with other parents. We were lucky in that we lived in a pretty small town with one medium-sized high school. This sometimes resulted in a call or comment from another parent. In other words, there were many sets of eyes in the community. (Remember, trust but verify.)

As described above, several of us from VTTI and the National Institutes of Health conducted a naturalistic driving study, putting unobtrusive cameras and sensors in the cars of 42 newly licensed teen drivers for 18 months. And yes, as a reminder, the teens volunteered to participate in the study. Using this instrumentation, which runs continuously while the car is on, we were able to classify the drivers into high, moderate, and low risk based on their involvement in crashes and near-crashes. We found that the highest risk group remained high risk, the moderate-risk group became low risk over time, and the low-risk group remained low risk the entire time.

How do you determine your teen's risk group classification? At the very least, you should be aware of the warning signs of a high-risk driver: Moving violations, car damage (even minor), even a car that is always locked in the garage. New technology is now available that allows parents or guardians to monitor their teens with sensors and even video while the teens drive. There are many companies out there that sell such systems and services. One of the oldest companies, DriveCam, has been around long enough to have some data available about the effectiveness of its systems. They claim a:

70% reduction in teen involvement in serious crashes and *more than 80% reduction* in injuries and fatalities for teens who have driver monitoring systems installed in their cars.

Now, these are claims of huge benefits. Even though the company undoubtedly makes an assumption here and there in its calculations, the risk reduction at some significant level is undeniable.

There are many driver monitoring systems available today. Some are very simple and measure speed, hard braking, and swerving, while others are quite sophisticated and have cameras. VTTI has developed a research-based monitoring system that is probably the most sophisticated but is currently too expensive to sell. However, I will describe all of its features so that you can get the full picture should you choose (wisely) to go shopping online for an available monitoring system.

The VTTI system, called Driver Coach, is designed to be able to detect all of the riskiest teen driving behaviors, including seat belt use, speeding, swerving, hard braking, fast accelerations, distraction, alcohol presence (a future capability of the system), and fatigue. My friend, colleague, and former student, Charlie Klauer, and I conceptualized an initial study using this system; Andy Petersen and his hardware folks at VTTI built the systems. This system only records video and sensor data when a certain threshold measure has been detected, such as the car traveling faster than 15 mph above the speed limit. If such a threshold is crossed, the system is triggered to record 12 seconds of video and sensor data that are then transmitted to a data reduction center at VTTI. The parents or guardians and the teen participating in the study then receive a report card every week with video clips and the driving behaviors of interest. In essence, the system allows you to *watch* your teen drive, similarly to when you are riding along with the teen.

As I have stated before, I have raised two teens and fully understand how excited your kids are going to be about having a system like this in their car. And I fully understand that such systems will mysteriously get broken or stolen from time to time. But two aspects may make this option more palatable:

1. The VTTI system, and some other driver monitoring systems, only record data when a threshold value is exceeded. That is, if your teen drives responsibly (no alcohol, no speeding, wearing a seat belt, no aggressive driving, no texting), you will never see anything about his or her driving.

2. VTTI is currently installing test systems in the cars of newly permitted drivers. In Virginia, this means that teen participants will have these systems in their cars for nine months before they start driving independently. The hope here is that these teen drivers will learn to drive such that the system never collects data, making it agreeable for the teens while teaching them to avoid the highest-risk driving situations.

I recommend seriously thinking about purchasing a driver monitoring system for your teens. If you search the Internet for "teen driver monitoring systems," you will see a wide range available. Video is probably very helpful, but those systems are more expensive. Some insurance companies, like American Family, are also starting driver monitoring programs that are fairly low cost. For Driver Coach, VTTI is experimenting with the "calculator model" in which the systems are loaned out for a year from the high school, and then returned and reused. In this case, the family would only have to pay a small monthly fee (maybe $9.99) for the service. Although not free, this option is cheaper than receiving just one speeding ticket during a year!

A critical point to make here is that, if you choose to buy a driver monitoring system, you have to actively participate in the entire program. Parents or guardians who look at the data provided each week and actively give feedback to their teens will reduce their teen's risk. Parents or guardians who do not actively look at data and do not provide feedback will not see much, if any, risk reduction.

The Highest Risk Scenario: The Tale of "Racer Live"

Since you understand the crash/cake ingredient simile and know the high-risk teen driving factors, I'll tell you a story that involves risk at an astronomical level.

We had a lifelong friend growing up named Bruce. Bruce was the ultimate gregarious extrovert. In other words, he was invariably the life of the party. Bruce earned his nickname "Racer Live" throughout his years. The "Live" part came from what you might expect. The "Racer" part started out, perhaps unexpectedly, as sarcasm by way of his older brother. Bruce's dad always had family projects, building something or doing home improvements. Bruce soon learned that if he kicked over the paint bucket enough times, his dad would ask less for his help.

The classic story was that, when Bruce was about 10 or so, his mother asked him to watch a pan of frying bacon while she ran across the street to borrow something from the neighbors. When she returned, she found the kitchen full of smoke, the pan on fire, and Bruce dutifully watching the spectacle. When she calmed down enough to ask what he was thinking, he simply responded that he did exactly as instructed and had continuously watched the bacon.

But Racer soon grew to love cars, motorcycles, speed, girls, and fun. In essence, he only continued to prove that his childhood nickname was accurate. One fateful night, Bruce was riding his 400 cc dirt bike home from a party with his girlfriend. He was moving at a rapid pace and drew the attention of a local sheriff in a rural community.

Bruce knew some dirt trails in the area, so rather than get into trouble, he decided to RUN FROM THE LAW. Let's recap: Bruce was a teen, was riding a motorcycle, was under the influence of alcohol, had a girl with him, and had plenty of testosterone. Throw in the fact that he was basically involved in a high-speed chase on a motorcycle, and you have all the ingredients present for a deadly recipe.

Now, boys and girls, there is an old saying about running from the law to which you should pay attention: "You can't outrun the Motorola," meaning the radio in every police car. Just so you know, radio waves travel at the speed of light, which could only be achieved by a dirt bike with an infinitely large engine. And few things make our good friends in law enforcement as tense as a high-speed chase. These things NEVER end well.

Well, Bruce did okay for a little while, but he soon slid off of the road on a sharp curve while traveling at more than 70 mph, narrowly missed some trees that certainly would have been fatal, and slid down a hill to a stop with the bike on top of him and the exhaust pipe burning his leg. As the sheriff came over the hill, he witnessed Bruce's girlfriend beating on him with her helmet. The officer apparently was in no particular hurry at that point to make what was the ultimate arrest. Fortunately, Bruce had one ingredient missing from his figurative cake that surely would have resulted in a fatal crash: He was wearing his signature stars and stripes helmet, which saved him from serious head injury caused by both the crash and his girlfriend.

Believe me when I tell you that I am not trying to glorify this behavior. Bruce was literally thousands of times at higher risk of dying during this episode than he was for the rest of his driving and riding career. It was just a momentary, very bad decision teens like Bruce make every day. For every story like this, there are a hundred that end with someone dead or permanently disabled. Bruce himself would be the first to punish any of his five daughters or any of his grandkids if they pulled a stunt like that. The only reason that Bruce avoided extended jail time and only had to pay hefty fines and lose his license is because the crash occurred during 1975 in rural Kentucky, not 2015 anywhere in the United States.

I tell this story both so that you will remember the key points of the risks involved with teens and to honor my friend Bruce. Bruce passed away in 2013 of unrelated causes at age 56. He was a very successful businessman; left behind a large, wonderful family; and was elected magistrate of his county. More than 1,000 people came to his funeral with story after story of how he changed their lives for the better. Many of them had made mistakes in their lives, and Bruce had given them a second chance like he had after that fateful night. I, and many, many others, are glad we did not lose him on that night when he was 17. Unfortunately, almost all of us know of someone who was not so lucky. How many lives could they have touched?

Bruce taking the wheel of a VW bus (of course) that was retrofitted with a bullhorn

General Resources

http://www.ncbi.nlm.nih.gov/pmc/articles/PMC3218800/

http://www.iihs.org/

http://www.nhtsa.gov/FARS

http://www.iihs.org/iihs/topics/laws/gdl_calculator

http://sleepfoundation.org/sleep-topics/teens-and-sleep

http://discover.umn.edu/news/teaching-education/students-grades-and-health-improve-later-high-school-start-times

http://www.lytx.com/our-markets/family/research-proven

https://www.aaafoundation.org/sites/default/files/NationwideReviewOfGDL.pdf

Romoser, M. R. E., Pollatsek, A., Fisher, D. L., & Williams, C. C. (2013). Comparing the glance patterns of older versus younger experienced drivers: Scanning for hazards while approaching and entering the intersection. *Transportation Research Part F, 16*, 104-116.

Pradhan, A. K., Pollatsek, A., Knodler, M. & Fisher, D. L. (2009). Can younger drivers be trained to scan for information that will reduce their risk in roadway traffic scenarios that are hard to identify as hazardous? *Ergonomics, 52*, 657-673.

Garay Vega, L., Fisher, D. L. & Pollatsek, A. (2007). Hazard anticipation of novice and experienced drivers: empirical evaluation on a driving simulator in daytime and nighttime conditions. *Transportation Research Record, 2009*, 1-7.

Li, K., Simons-Morton, B. G., Vaca, F. E., & Hingson, R. (2014). Association between riding with an impaired driver and driving while impaired. *Pediatrics, 144*(4), 620-626.

Thomas, F. D., Korbelak, K. T., Divekar, G. U., Blomberg, R. D., Romoser, M. R. E., & Fisher, D. L. (2013). *Evaluation of a New Approach to Training Hazard Anticipation Skills of Young Drivers*. Washington, DC: National Highway Traffic Safety Administration.

Chapter 9.

Senior Drivers:
Rage Against the Dying of the Light

My wife, Melissa, and I have had two parents who lived long enough to have to give up driving. My father had to give up this privilege due to a series of strokes, while Melissa's mother gave up driving due to poor eyesight caused by macular degeneration.

I was fortunate to be able to help my father after his strokes since he moved into an assisted living facility close to my house. At that stage, he had lost his mobility to the point where he couldn't walk without some assistance. The damage caused by his strokes was such that his vision and balance were impaired. Even then, losing his independence was very hard. I recall one time when I took him to the local grocery store to do some weekly shopping. As I often did, I parked by the curb at the store, helped him into a motorized shopping cart, and then went to park the car while he waited. Normally, I would then accompany him into the store, helping him get around and find what he needed. This time, however, my father decided to exercise his independence.

As I was parking the car, I saw him look around, and, with a wry smile on his face, he took off on his cart and into the store without me. I was a little freaked out, envisioning finding him under a pile of soup cans or mowing over a group of fellow shoppers. As I parked and ran into the store, however, I found him cruising around in the wine aisle, putting bottles in his basket. The bad news for him was that he could no longer drink because of his medications. But, he was a good sport as I put the wine bottles back and we continued to shop. I tried to point out the risks involved in what he had done. In the end, though, I couldn't really scold my father, and we had a good laugh about it.

It is very, very hard to give up one's mobility. In essence, that person is losing some degree of independence. Even with the more widespread availability of public transit, rides from family and friends, and the resources to call a cab when needed, there is less independence offered than being able to hop in one's own car and go whenever, and wherever, you choose. My mother-in-law, Nancy, told me that no senior would buy my book because I would just tell them they can't drive. So, I took her comment to heart and decided to focus here on:

1. Why older drivers are safer than you think.

2. How to help us all drive longer.

VTTI performed a study several years ago during which we had younger and older drivers react to an imminent crash event. We found that, unsurprisingly, the younger drivers had faster reaction times to hitting the brakes. However, the older drivers were able to stop in a slightly shorter distance. How is that possible, you may ask? Well, the younger drivers were quick to get a foot on the brake, but then they hesitated for a brief moment while they decided the best course of action, such as steering instead of, or in addition to, braking. Even though it took them longer to get to the brakes, older drivers hit those brakes hard and without hesitation. Maybe because of experience, maybe because they knew on some level they needed to compensate or adapt, the end result was that the older drivers were more effective at making an emergency stop.

From societal and public safety perspectives, there's not an older driver problem. Seniors (aged 74+) are consistently at the *lowest crash risk* of all driving age groups on a *per licensed driver basis*. One reason for this lowered risk is that older drivers generally adapt very well, for a very long time, despite growing limitations in vision, cognition, motor skills, reaction time, and/or physical flexibility.

Note, however, that I wrote older drivers crash less *per licensed driver*. Older drivers tend to drive substantially fewer miles than younger age groups. When you look at the individual skill level and from the perspective of the older driver, it is more instructive to look at the crash rate *per mile driven*. In that case, we see what is known as the "bathtub" curve, with seniors mirroring the high crash rates seen in the youngest and least experienced drivers.

It is interesting to note that some in our field believe that the higher crash rate per mile traveled for seniors owes largely to those seniors who actually travel very few miles due to either the roads they frequent and/or their individual levels of impairment and risk. Of course, at some point, drivers who live long enough can no longer adapt. It may be that the older drivers who crash the most simply can no longer compensate by driving on slower and safer roads, in limited traffic, in good weather, in daylight, etc.

Another point to consider relative to injurious and fatal crash rates is how we age, both individually and as a population. As we get older, we get more fragile with respect to surviving a fall or a car crash. This means that, whatever the crash risk, the risk of sustaining a serious injury or a fatality is far greater per crash among older drivers compared to younger drivers. Therefore, we need to both prevent crashes using a variety of countermeasures and to continue making vehicles not only crashworthy but crashworthy in a way that specifically helps the aging driver and his or her passenger.

Mobility is a big concern. We are an aging society and are projected to continue to age as a population well into the middle of this century. Whatever issues we see on the road today will be even greater challenges tomorrow. Additionally, those of us of the baby-boomer generation who are currently creating a "grey tsunami" will likely be fundamentally different than our parents and grandparents in terms of a wide variety of factors that may impact driving safety. Those factors can include general health and vigor, driving patterns, living conditions, level and desire for activity, acceptance of technology, etc.

How do we keep us all mobile? My friend and colleague, Jon Antin, directs the Center for Vulnerable Road User Safety at VTTI. This center studies younger and older drivers, as well as those who are largely unprotected in the transportation community, such as pedestrians and bicyclists. I asked Jon to help develop a few key points about older, or more mature, drivers. Here are a number of possibilities that might help in the near or longer term:

1. Connected/automated vehicles.

   I will discuss this new generation of vehicle technology later in Chapter 11. In a nutshell, these evolving technologies may significantly help older drivers to drive by providing automated assistance on a number of levels. Assuming, of course, that such systems are *well designed* with the older driver in mind.

2. Emergence of "livable communities" and an increase in well-designed, shared roadway spaces.

   These options not only apply to the general transportation population, including bicyclists and pedestrians; they could also be applied to senior drivers.

3. Brain training.

   There is some strong evidence for the successful impact of "brain exercises" on senior driving safety. One such study was the Advanced Cognitive Training for Independent and Vital Elderly (ACTIVE) trial. This study assessed the effectiveness of three "brain exercise" programs in improving the cognitive performance of older persons. VTTI is literally in the middle of finalizing data collection and analyzing data from our naturalistic studies that will help inform this very topic. Dr. Antin expects we will soon find some positive results regarding the benefits of both physical training and driver training among the older driver population.

4. Improving useful field of view.

   Useful field of view is the degree to which you can process driving-relevant information in your peripheral vision. Unfortunately, your useful field of view declines with age, thus impacting driving. The field of view that you can practically use has been the most successful way to predict any meaningful outcomes in real-world driving safety. The good news is that new evidence suggests you can improve your useful field-of-view functionality through practice and "exercises." It may be true that, by "exercising" your useful field of view, you can reduce your crash risk and be mobile longer.

Notice that I avoided talking about when to quit driving. First, there is no formula; functional age varies greatly from person to person. A person in his or her 90s could drive more safely than another person who is 70 years old. Secondly, there is a vast amount of information out there to help older drivers gauge their driving ability, such as the AARP website or the AAA Senior Driving website. Of course, this means that the senior driver needs to be able to use the Internet or enlist someone who can. Third, I want Nancy and other senior drivers to buy my book. Not out of greed, but out of a desire to ensure they have good tools and resources needed to enhance their driving safety.

General Resources

http://www.aarp.org

http://seniordriving.aaa.com/evaluate-your-driving-ability

http://www.ncbi.nlm.nih.gov/pmc/articles/PMC4055506/

http://www.ncbi.nlm.nih.gov/pmc/articles/PMC2916176/

http://bit.ly/1TEDCae

http://bit.ly/1CFD3J7

Chapter 10.

Motorcycles and a
Few Tips for Motorcyclists

When I was a junior in high school in Rochester, Minnesota, my father got transferred to Atlanta, Georgia. We had some debate about whether I would tag along or just finish high school. I had a girlfriend, friends, etc. and wasn't too excited about starting over in a new school. I ended up moving. The caveat was that my father would give me $1,000 and his motorcycle at the end of the school year, and I could travel anywhere I wanted all summer long. I rode 4,000 miles and spent less time in Minnesota than you might think, because by that time my girlfriend had left me for one of my best friends (sigh). I was 17 and, oddly enough, the trip didn't seem nearly as crazy as it does today. A lot of my friends had bikes. We often commuted on bikes to save gas and have fun. A few years of racing dirt bikes made me a pretty safe rider because I always assumed that hitting the pavement would lead to my own fatality, which was a pretty good assumption.

Overall, I had some close calls with motorcycles that taught me a lot about things like conspicuity, but I never had a crash.

However, I would never, never, never let my kids do what I did.

Why am I so wary of letting my kids and other young people on a motorcycle? It's simple: The odds for motorcyclists are, by far, the highest that we see among all transportation users (meaning cars, trucks, etc.):

Per mile traveled, motorcyclists are *more than 30 times more likely* to die in a motorcycle crash than in a car crash.

If you ride a sports bike (think leaning forward and going fast, such as an Interceptor, Ninja, GSX-R, etc.), you are *more than 100 times more likely* per mile traveled to die in a motorcycle crash than in a car crash.

This is why some in the driving safety business don't call them motorcycles; they call them donorcycles. But hey, we're all adults (or soon will be), and motorcycles are fun. You can make your own decisions, and I might need a kidney someday.

In all seriousness, though, I could write an entire book about how to control and reduce risk on a motorcycle (which might happen if y'all like this book). Experience on a bike helps, assuming you can survive that long. Training probably helps, particularly programs that are comprehensive and teach defensive riding techniques. But the real "biggies" in terms of motorcycle risk are discussed below. To help me with this section, I asked one of the VTTI motorcycle safety experts, Shane McLaughlin, to weigh in with a few tips. Shane is a friend, former student, and colleague who heads the VTTI Motorcycle Research Group.

Recognize How Bikes are Different

Very few motorcyclists can brake as hard, or swerve as dramatically, as they can in a car. Just assume that you are not one of those "very few." If you ride a motorcycle like you drive a car, you're going to get into trouble. After a crash in a car, the discussion is usually about vehicle insurance, sometimes health insurance. With a similar crash on a motorcycle, that ensuing discussion is more likely to be about disability or life insurance. On a motorcycle, you have to avoid the crash altogether through a series of protective measures.

Know Your Riding Proficiency

22% of riders involved in fatal crashes **do not have a valid motorcycle license.**

Some of these riders have had their licenses revoked, but others just never bothered to get licensed. This means such riders are undoubtedly less proficient. Even if you have trained (highly recommended) and have a proper license, each time you get on your motorcycle, think about how long it has been since you last rode. Think about how polished you are and what might need some work or practice. Consider the extra tasks involved in riding a motorcycle compared to driving a car. For example, if you are looking for traffic as you approach an intersection while on a motorcycle, can you do so while down-shifting, balancing, reading signs and signals, and braking smoothly? If it has been a while since you've been on your bike, put in the necessary practice (it makes perfect, after all). If you're riding with friends, pick ones who will accommodate the pace you need to maintain your safety.

Turns Will Get You

A major source of injuries and fatalities for motorcycle riders is going too fast while taking a turn. Keep in mind that you are the only person who can avoid this mistake, so it's critical that you maintain awareness of your speed. Riders need to know the road, read every sign, and eliminate extra speed before needing to lean. Think through what layers of protection you have. Consider how you will manage hazards, such as how far you will stay from the lane boundaries, if you could swerve away from gravel in your lane, and if you can see far enough through the curve to stop while turning.

I Brake for Safety

Braking can generally get you out of many common crash scenarios. For example, if a line of cars stops in front of you, there's a good chance you will need to brake very hard. So, how good are you at braking on a motorcycle? Part of this goes back to riding proficiency and knowing your bike. You need to allow enough following distance based on your level of riding abilities. Arguing about the contribution of the front brake is like arguing about gravity; if you are not using that brake, you're braking well below the capabilities of the bike. It's easy enough to get up to speed, but how prepared will you be if you need to stop suddenly?

They Don't See You

We often assume when we drive our cars through an intersection that other drivers see us and will obey the traffic laws. Although it's always good to be an alert and attentive driver, this is a pretty good assumption to make. Even if you are wrong, you have a lot of steel, plastic, airbags, and seat belts to protect you.

None of this is true for a motorcycle.

Even though most riders often believe motorcycles should be easy to see, they are a lot less conspicuous than you might think due to a variety of factors ranging from their profiles to the color of the bike and the rider's clothing to their contrast with the background environment.

Here is some advice to increase your chances of being seen by other drivers:

1. Always assume other drivers don't see you and that they are about to pull out, change lanes, or otherwise encroach on your space. Always be aware of the closest threats in space and time, and look ahead to determine where you can go if a driver encroaches on your path. In other words, be vigilant, remain suspicious of other drivers, and have an out.

2. Do everything you can to increase your conspicuity. Burn your lights, buy a brightly colored bike, add reflective tape to your bike, buy a kit that flashes your lights, wear reflective clothing, wear light-colored clothing, and buy a brightly colored helmet. You need to actively work at being conspicuous.

Just Because You Can, Doesn't Mean You Should, Part 2

We should ban all helmets in college football and the NFL

Sound crazy? Not as crazy, my friend, as 31 states getting rid of motorcycle helmet laws. Are you kidding me?

photo by Jean Paul Talledo Vilela

If you are ever flying through the air at 60 mph, I'll bet you wish you had one. But hey, just because it is legal doesn't mean that you have to do it, so be a real rebel and wear a helmet. And not just a cereal bowl with a strap on it (like the one pictured to your right); wear a real helmet. That way, fellas, your wife/girlfriend/mother/significant other won't have to clean up drool and your ass (hopefully in that order) for the rest of your miserable life, assuming you even survive a crash without a helmet.

And if that last part sounds sexist, it's because 91% of motorcycle fatalities are men; the majority of the other 9% are women passengers. Remember what the most dangerous, mind-altering substance is for driving? It's doubly true for riding motorcycles: Testosterone!

Wearing a helmet *reduces your odds of dying in a crash by almost 40%.*

That means four more helmeted riders would survive every 10 fatal crashes where no helmet is present.

139

Natural Selection: Riding under the Influence

Our friends at the Motorcycle Safety Foundation estimate that:

You are about *40 times more likely* (odds = 40.0) to be in a fatal motorcycle crash if you have consumed even a moderate amount of alcohol (blood alcohol content, or BAC, greater than 0.05%).

A BAC of 0.05% is not very high. For me, a male at 185 pounds, that means I can't have more than two beers in the first hour and one beer per hour after that. To ride safely, I need to be well below that limit, meaning no more than one beer, period.

Just to emphasize this point: If I am riding a sports bike while sober, I am already at *100 times greater risk* of a crash. That risk *increases by 40 times* if I drink a couple of beers. In big, round numbers (keeping in mind that calculating your risk is not as simple as exact multiplication):

Per mile traveled, you are in the neighborhood of *4,000 times more likely* to die in a crash on your sports bike after a couple of drinks compared to driving a car while sober.

Hence the title of this section: Riding drunk, particularly on a motorcycle, is just a matter of natural selection.

Make Sure Your Mid-life Crisis is Really Mid-life

During the last 10 years or so, a scary statistic has emerged for the older rider population:

***75% of fatal motorcycle crashes* involve riders over the age of 40.**

The older rider group is made up of several different kinds of cats: Those who have been riding for a long time, those who are new to riding, and those who used to ride but haven't for a long time. It appears that a lot of these older rider fatal crashes, or at least the reason for the growth in the fatality rate, fall within the third group: Those who haven't been on a ride for a long time but started riding again. There are probably several factors at play here, including rusty skills, overconfidence, buying a more powerful or bigger bike, and age-related performance degradation. The key here is to ease back into riding. It is important to re-train, consider yourself a novice, and take things slower than you used to...at least until you've re-developed your skill level.

Group Riding: Are You the Weakest Link?

Another phenomenon appears as a significant risk factor during group riding: Crashes involving the least experienced rider in the group. Obviously, more experienced riders have the skills necessary to ride faster, take curves faster, stop faster, etc. However, the least experienced riders in the group may be pushing beyond their skill levels to keep up with the group. If you are an experienced rider, be cognizant of various skill levels in your group and don't put your less-experienced buddy in a bad situation. If you are the more inexperienced rider, recognize that other riders may make it look easy. Don't let the moment you run off the road be the time you realize you're not as strong of a rider. Ride within your comfort level; you can catch up a little later.

A Special Case of Speed Kills

When I lived in Colorado, I had a Honda "750 four" (as in, four cylinders). Each year, some friends and I would get together and take a bike trip around the mountains. This, of course, was a lot of fun.

During one of these trips, we pulled off at a rest stop to hang out for a bit. While merging back onto the nearly empty interstate, we were feeling our oats a bit and decided to accelerate to well over 100 mph, something that wasn't hard to do with the bikes we had.

As we came over a rise, we saw a state policeman sitting on an overpass. A short time later, we were all pulled over on the side of the road and were convinced we were going to jail. The implications of going 55 mph over the speed limit vary by state, but they are always expensive and not pretty. The officer came up and asked, "Do you know the speed limit?" I said "Yes, sir, it's 55." He said "Well, I got you going 70 and your friend here going 75..."

We all breathed a huge sigh of relief because we knew he was guessing and didn't get us on radar. But then he said "Boys, this is your lucky day. I myself have a Honda CBX 1050 [a six-cylinder bike], and I am sure that you were surprised that you were speeding. So I am just going to give you a warning this time...but I will radio ahead, and we will all be keeping an eye on you." Funny thing was, we thought he was just trying to scare us, only to see state patrol cars flash their lights at us two other times that day. It was a good thing we were going close to the speed limit. A lucky day, indeed.

As this story illustrates, motorcycles can be wickedly fast. And our bikes were nowhere close to what you can buy today. As an example, the new 650 hp Chevy Corvette Z06 can go from 0 to 60 mph in 2.95 seconds. Unless you are willing to pay hundreds of thousands of dollars, this Corvette is the fastest production car, and it's damned fast. By contrast, there are 11 production motorcycles that are *faster*, including two that can move from 0 to 60 mph in the sub-2.5-second range. It takes very, very little time to get into trouble on a bike.

Near my house in Southwest Virginia, we typically see kids from the nearby college ride along our curvy (meaning, fun for them) road on their sports bikes during the spring. When my kids were young and playing near the road, these kids on their sports bikes zoomed by at speeds in the triple digits. It made me want an offensive weapon every now and again. Every year, one or two disabling injuries or fatalities happen among sports bike riders on that road. Not only does the road feature sharp curves, but it has suburban neighborhoods, hidden driveways, short sight distances, and slow traffic.

As you might expect, speeding on a bike is a factor in a large percentage of fatal crashes. Specifically:

34% of motorcycle fatalities **involve speeding, compared to 22% for cars and 8% for heavy trucks.**

Stay at a reasonable speed, no matter how tempting it is to let 'er fly.

A motorcycle instrumented by VTTI researchers to capture naturalistic riding behaviors is displayed for guests, including former U.S. Secretary of Transportation Ray LaHood; photo by Logan Wallace

General Resources

http://www.iihs.org/iihs/topics/t/motorcycles/fatalityfacts/motorcycles

http://www-nrd.nhtsa.dot.gov/Pubs/812035.pdf

http://isddc.dot.gov/OLPFiles/NHTSA/013695.pdf

http://www.iii.org/issue-update/motorcycle-crashes

http://www.ghsa.org/html/stateinfo/laws/helmet_laws.html

http://bit.ly/1V6KIpB

http://www.ghsa.org/html/issues/motorcyclesafety.html

http://www.msf-usa.org/downloads/Alcohol_Awareness.pdf

http://www.ghsa.org/html/files/pubs/spotlights/motorcycles_2012.pdf

http://bit.ly/1BJO8Ci

Chapter 11.

The Crystal Ball:
Be Ready for the Future

We have all seen visions of what driving will be like in the future. Most of those visions are informed by the flying cars in "The Jetsons," "Back to the Future," or a 1950s *Saturday Evening Post* ad (above) showing a car driving itself while a family plays games under a clear glass dome.

There are many advantages to such a vision. There will be less traffic, and we can be productive or entertained while we commute. And, hey, if we can just get rid of all of the human drivers, we will all be safe, right? You may be surprised by my answer.

But first, a little about the progression of new vehicle technologies.

Active Safety Systems

As discussed earlier in this book, the cars of today represent amazing feats of engineering. One recent feat is the effective design of *active* safety systems, or crash avoidance systems. Simply stated, *passive* safety systems include seat belts, airbags, crumple zones, etc. that help you survive a crash. By contrast, *active* safety systems help you avoid a crash.

In 1991, I helped conduct the first on-road evaluation of an active safety system concept known as forward collision warning. Dan McGehee, now at the University of Iowa, was a student of mine who wrote his master's thesis from this study. We instrumented a prototype Cadillac with a $15,000 scanning laser from a jet fighter; this laser served as the warning sensor. (Today, automotive radars sell for just a few hundred dollars and are much more capable.)

The study was conducted on-road with a participant who was a novice to the scenario. The driver was told to follow a car ahead that "was also testing a variety of advanced technologies." The lead vehicle, however, was just leading the route and braking at different levels and speeds so we could see how our participant driver reacted. Because we didn't have much money to conduct the study, we had a mannequin in the passenger seat of the participant's vehicle serving as the car's "experimenter." We ended up winning a best paper award from a journal (kind of a big deal for academics) for this and several other studies that showed potential benefits of such an active system, both in terms of headway selection and brake reaction time.

My friend and colleague, Rich Deering, spent many years at General Motors (GM) doing safety research and design work for safety systems, including the early days of active safety systems. Of course, various suppliers and inventors would talk to Rich on a regular basis, trying to sell their active safety ideas to a very large vehicle manufacturer and get wealthy in the process by selling hundreds of thousands of units. Rich used to say on a pretty regular basis that he had a good week because he knew how to solve more than 100% of the crash problem. You may ask, "How could that be true?" Well, it wasn't. But the claims of the inventors and suppliers ("This will reduce rear-end crashes by 50%," or "That will reduce run-off-road crashes by 70%") added up to more than was even possible. The lesson here, which will be discussed in detail later, is to be careful about the source of what people tell you, particularly regarding new technology. Treat claims with suspicion, consider the source, and be a little skeptical.

With that in mind, here is some information about how to make the most of active safety systems.

Become one with your ride

Active safety systems include collision warning systems, like the forward collision warning system described above, and even limited control through automated braking. The results are still preliminary as to how effective these systems are at reducing injurious crashes. However, our friends at the Insurance Institute for Highway Safety (IIHS) tell us the following:

1. **Electronic stability control (ESC) is very effective and *reduces fatal crashes by about one-third* compared to non-equipped cars.**

    ESC essentially automatically controls the power, braking, and wheel slip of each wheel independently. By performing these maneuvers at a high rate of speed, the system can stabilize a car that is sliding or otherwise losing traction, for example.

2. **Forward collision warnings *reduce injurious crashes by about 15%*, but the results vary by manufacturer.**

    Systems that automatically brake at some level at the onset of a forward collision scenario, instead of just warning the driver, seem to be more effective.

3. **The results of road/lane departure warnings and adaptive headlights also vary by manufacturer.**

    In these cases, there is some evidence that some systems may have a detrimental effect on the driver. As talked about several times in this book, you need a *well-designed* system, so pay attention to the details of the IIHS and others when buying a car.

Active safety systems are continually evolving and will clearly improve with each model year as more becomes known about them. However, one thing is certain regarding active safety technology: You need to understand how the system works and what it is telling you. Simpler systems of the past may have allowed you to "fly by the seat of the pants" after you left the dealership, having been completely uninterested in what the salesman was trying to tell you and instead quickly signing the papers so you could get the car on the road for a spin. Newer technologies, however, require that you be patient and take a little time to learn the active safety features.

Even though we all know that pretty much NO ONE reads the owner's manual of a vehicle, you may want to take the time to do so for newer cars. That's because many studies designed to determine how drivers use new systems over the years have shown that the systems could become ineffective and even detrimental. This happens when the driver has an incorrect *mental model* of how a system works. My friend and colleague at VTTI, Eddy Llaneras, has conducted dozens of such studies, including research into a backup warning system available in new cars.

During one particular study, a driver would receive a backup warning and even an automated brake to avoid the scenario. The driver would look around, and, upon not seeing any obstacle, would continue to back up despite the fact that he or she had received a warning. The problem in this scenario is that you can't see small objects or children behind many larger vehicles, which is why the warning system activated in the first place. In effect, the system correctly detected an obstacle behind the vehicle, the system warned the driver, but the driver backed over the object anyway. The solution was then to suggest that a backup camera become part of the warning system, a configuration that will soon be required on all new cars. However, you should keep in mind that the effectiveness of such a solution depends on whether drivers actually use and rely upon this rear-vision system. As with all new vehicle technologies designed to help the driver, if the systems aren't used—and aren't used *properly*—the driver will not see any benefits.

The overall point here is to learn how the system works enough that you can work *with it* to avoid crashes.

Be aware of unintended consequences

Much of the work performed at VTTI centers on testing new technologies for manufacturers, their suppliers, and even on behalf of government agencies. A big part of this testing is determining if there are any *unintended consequences* that arise when people actually use the systems in the real world.

As an example, a truck manufacturer built a system a number of years ago that would provide the driver with an alert when he or she was about to cross a lane line on the highway. This manufacturer was marketing the system as part of a drowsiness monitoring system with the intent that, once drivers received an alert, they would find a good spot to pull over and rest. However, the manufacturer actually found during the first field tests that drivers were not using the system as an indicator to pull over and rest; they were using the system as an "alarm clock." That is, drivers liked the system because they knew that the system would wake them when they were tired and falling asleep. This usage also allowed the drivers to cover more mileage than before. The problem here was that the system did nothing to warn drivers of objects ahead. Once in a while, the system would also "miss" an alert. This over-reliance on the system was an unintended consequence that could well have actually *increased* crashes for that particular system. Luckily, that system was never deployed in such a configuration.

I bring this up because you need to be aware of your behavior as you use active safety systems, even when you understand how they work. An important part of understanding is using the systems as they were meant to be used and not over-relying on them to perform duties that fall outside of what they were designed to do.

The Next Big Thing: Cars that Talk to Each Other and Everything Else

Modern cars are essentially rolling computers. Thanks to GPS, they often know where they are, what direction they are heading, and their speed. Positions measured by an automotive GPS are not terribly accurate, though, with errors as great as 30 feet relative to absolute position (that is, the ground). However, if two cars were to travel close together and talk to the same GPS satellites, their position *relative to one another* would be pretty accurate. Essentially, if you could make cars that "talk" to each other, they could avoid hitting each other, or at least send warnings about impending collisions.

This concept is actually a reality and is called connected-vehicle communications. This type of communication uses dedicated short-range radios, which are essentially a new version of WiFi, to enable vehicles to talk to each other, the roadside, and devices that include smartphones. Connected-vehicle communications have huge potential. Using it, your car can instantly sense when the car in front of you slams on its brakes. It can just as easily sense when the vehicle five cars ahead of you slams on its brakes. Connected-vehicle communications can also tell you when you are about to change lanes into another car or when you should slow down due to hazardous road conditions.

With roadside radios and even radios embedded in cell phones, connected-vehicle communications can tell you when you are about to run a stop light; when another car is about to run a stop light; when there is a motorcycle in your blind spot (more conspicuity!); and/or when you are on a collision path with a bicycle, scooter, or pedestrian. The safety possibilities using connected-vehicle communications are vast. Perhaps the most beautiful part of connected-vehicle communications is that you get all of these safety benefits for the cost of a relatively inexpensive radio, compared to the more expensive radar, sonar, and machine-vision (that is, camera-based) sensors.

My friend, former student, and colleague, Zac Doerzaph, directs the VTTI Center for Advanced Automotive Research. He has been working with connected-vehicle technology for more than a decade. He and his group have done a number of studies that show the huge potential of this technology. It is estimated by our friends at the National Highway Traffic Safety Administration (NHTSA) that:

Connected-vehicle technology can help *eliminate about 70% of crashes* involving alert drivers.

That is why NHTSA has been working in conjunction with car companies and suppliers for a long time and is considering issuing a rule that all new cars have to be equipped with connected-vehicle capabilities in the near future.

Connected motorcycle at VTTI;
from the author's personal photo collection

Humans and Automated-vehicle Technologies

"Free the hands, free the mind"

Years ago, my friend, Jim, who worked in a ski resort in Colorado, talked me into trying snowboarding instead of skiing. There are a number of interesting expressions associated with snowboarding, like "The shredder the better," or "Dude! Rip it, don't strip it" (referring to the powder). However, the one expression I remember well also applies to this book: "Free the hands, free the mind." In snowboarding, this advice refers to the existential experience of having only one device (the board) to carve the slope as opposed to the two boards and two poles (much less elegant) required in skiing. However, in the context of driving, the quote takes on a different meaning: If you are not engaged in controlling the vehicle, chances are you will not be engaged in driving at all.

Did we learn anything from Three Mile Island?

As I mentioned earlier, I had a good friend named Gene Farber who worked in driving safety as an engineer at Ford for many years. Gene was an iconic figure who influenced a lot of folks in our field, including me, for several reasons. First, he was a very bright pragmatist who valued science that could be applied in whatever form to saving lives, including car design, driver education, and coherent safety laws. Second, like Rich Deering (mentioned previously), Gene was a great "BS detector," which is important in our business. Everyone knows how to solve the driving safety problem, only most of the so-called solutions don't work. Third, Gene had a great sense of humor and could throw the BS card in a way that was both entertaining and acceptable.

One example of Gene's influence has stuck with me for the past 20 years. Gene was the chair of a large industry association safety committee. We had just heard a presentation about an automated-vehicle concept during which the car would essentially drive itself under most conditions and most of the time. Thus, the driver could give control to a car that would steer, maintain speed, and brake if needed. The driver's sole task was to be alert and watch in case something unusual happened, at which time the driver would need to take control back from the vehicle. At the end of the talk, Gene made a very simple and influential statement: "Are you crazy? The driver is not going to be ready to take control; in fact, they are going to be having sex in the back seat."

Gene's elegant point was this: We learned many years ago, through the nuclear power industry and elsewhere, that humans are terrible at staying alert and monitoring for something that rarely happens. We will soon see vehicles in large numbers that have varying degrees of automated control. These systems are starting to include sensors that monitor the state of the driver, but there is a cautionary tale here. As with active safety systems, you need to understand how your car works to a more advanced extent, understand when it works and when it doesn't, understand what it is telling you, and understand your role and responsibility in different situations.

Autonomous Vehicles

The rise of the automated vehicle

Engineers of all kinds are talking about the promise of vehicles that are automated (that is, vehicles that have some level of automation) and fully autonomous (what we consider fully self-driving). They often discuss the convenience afforded by automated vehicles; some talk about how more than 90% of crashes are caused, at least in part, by driver error, which is true. They will share anecdotes about how someone they know or someone they saw did something outrageous on the road that ended in disaster.

I believe that in our lifetime, or at least maybe yours, we will see the evolution of automation in vehicles continue to the point where cars drive themselves, more or less. These cars, at least initially, will likely be limited to certain roadways (such as highways) and scenarios (such as good weather) where myriad necessary sensors and systems can operate effectively.

My friend, former student, and colleague, Myra Blanco, runs the VTTI Center for Automated Vehicle Systems. She and her colleagues are making tremendous headway into the study of automated vehicles, from human factors to cybersecurity concerns. Myra will be among the first to tell you about impressive and innovative advances made around the world in the field of automated vehicles. She will point to other technological and societal changes that indicate the next generation of drivers may not even want to drive, or they likely won't need a license, because they can get more done by riding in an automated car than by driving a manual one. She will also talk about how young people probably will not even want their own cars in the future based on current trends in car sharing.

I do want to provide some food for thought regarding the evolution of automated vehicles. I believe there will continue to be manual driving in the transportation community, at least for the next few decades and maybe forever. What we'll likely see during that time is a mix of legacy vehicles traveling the same roads as automated vehicles. Why do I think this?

1. 43% of drivers in the U.S. commute less than 20 minutes to work. For such drivers, the question may become: Why spend extra money on an automated vehicle for such a short drive?

2. Even if automation was available today, it would take about 25 years for the current vehicle fleet in the U.S. to turn over so that most vehicles are automated.

3. Many in the U.S. can't afford or choose not to buy a new car. Will such drivers be able to purchase a car that costs more due to its automated features?

4. Some people simply enjoy driving. For example, even though automatic transmissions have been around for 70 years, the number of vehicles purchased with manual transmissions is the highest it has been in more than a decade.

5. 35% of roadways in the U.S. are unpaved. It's hard for an automated vehicle to follow lane lines when there aren't any.

Interestingly enough, our friends at the University of Michigan Transportation Research Institute recently released some initial findings that indicate motion sickness may be a factor to watch regarding fully autonomous vehicles. Based on their survey of 3,255 adult drivers in the U.S., China, India, Japan, the U.K., and Australia, up to 10% of drivers in the U.S. alone would be expected to "often, usually, or always experience some level of motion sickness." The survey also found that 23% of American adults would choose not to ride in a fully self-driving vehicle.

So, while we ponder the future of transportation, here are some things to consider when looking into that crystal ball...

An alert, attentive driver is very good at avoiding crashes

My friend, Gene Farber, also used to model driving behavior. He built a model that showed an average U.S. driver will make approximately three million successful braking maneuvers *with one failure* (a rear-end crash) during 25 years of driving. The drivers will successfully brake in all kinds of weather and lighting conditions, in numerous odd and anomalous scenarios during which other drivers do strange things, and on a range of road types. This should make you think that, whatever automated system is designed, it has to be very, very reliable and perform much better than the average driver to be truly effective.

Early in my career, I worked at the University of Iowa with high-fidelity driving simulators. These simulators allowed us to create any scenario we wanted with traffic doing whatever we wanted. In one case, we were trying to determine whether a radar-based forward crash avoidance system would be beneficial in helping distracted drivers avoid crashes. So, we distracted the driver and created a "reveal" scenario during which a simulated lead truck would suddenly swerve out of the lane, revealing a stationary car in the driver's lane. Based on everything that we knew about driver performance, such as reaction time, we calculated that at least one-half of the drivers could not possibly avoid the crash. After running 50 or more drivers through the scenario, *nobody crashed*. They avoided hitting the stopped vehicle by a number of methods, including swerving to the shoulder and not braking, slowing to let a vehicle pass in the adjacent lane and swerving left, and just hitting the brakes faster than expected. The moral of the story is: Don't underestimate an alert, attentive driver.

Example simulator; from the author's personal photo collection

What does this mean to you? If you are alert and attentive (and sober, etc.), you are a beast of crash avoidance, reducing your odds of crashing at every turn! By contrast, drivers cannot be relied upon to monitor and react under automated driving like they can in manual driving. Even if they're not having sex in the back seat, drivers will be reading, writing, and doing other things while the car drives itself. My friend, Eddy Llaneras, and other colleagues have shown that drivers take their eyes off the road for as much as *30 seconds in even partially automated driving*. To put that into perspective, it takes a little more than three seconds to travel the length of a football field at highway speeds; taking your eyes off of the road for 30 seconds is, well, completely out of touch.

What this all means is that automated vehicles have to be able to operate at a very high level to be acceptable and safe. The cars need to not only reliably understand what is going on around them; they also need to understand the state of the driver. If a system fails, it has to fail in a way that gives the driver plenty of time (maybe well over 10 seconds) to take control. In other words, these systems have to be very, very reliable and robust to any roadway, traffic, and driver scenario.

On a related note, automated systems always have been, and always will be, held to a much higher safety standard than manual cars *in cases during which the driver is not in control*. For example, if there is a multiple car crash in California, it rarely makes even the local news unless a lot of people died or traffic was really bad. By contrast, if an automated car goes haywire and crashes into a lot of other cars, it will be on four or more 24-hour cycles of CNN and every other news agency that will try to figure out what happened and what is being done about it.

So, autonomous vehicles will come sooner or later, but we have a ways to go…

photo courtesy of VTTI

General Resources

http://www.iihs.org/

http://www.iihs.org/iihs/sr/statusreport/article/45/6/5

http://bit.ly/1coYltL

http://www.wired.com/2014/02/feds-v2v/

http://www.nhtsa.gov/people/injury/research/udashortrpt/background.html

http://factfinder.census.gov

Edmunds.com, 2012

Dingus, T. A., McGehee, D. V., Manakkal, N., Jahns, S. K., Carney, C., & Hankey, J. (1997). Human factors field evaluation of automotive headway maintenance/collision warning devices. *Human Factors, 39*(2), 216-229.

Farber, E. & Paley, M. (1993). *Using freeway traffic data to estimate the effectiveness of rear end collision countermeasures.* Paper presented at the Third Annual IVHS America Meeting, IVHS America, Washington, DC.

Llaneras, R. E., Salinger, J., & Green, C. A. (2013). Human factors issues associated with limited ability autonomous driving systems: Drivers' allocation of visual attention to the forward roadway. In *Proceedings of the 7th International Driving Symposium on Human Factors in Driver Assessment, Training and Vehicle Design* (pp. 92-98).

Sivak, M. & Schoettle, B. (2015). *Motion Sickness in Self-Driving Vehicles* (Report No. UMTRI-2015-12). Ann Arbor, MI: University of Michigan Transportation Research Institute.

Final Thoughts:

Question What You Read and Hear

In some ways, driving safety is a funny business. Those of us in the business have our fair share of quirks. One thing you have to understand is that our data fluctuate, just as with many aspects of science. There are always new risks to analyze. New information continuously becomes available to enhance our current data. For instance, texting on a cell wasn't necessarily a risk even 10 years ago, and browsing on a cell wasn't even possible until a few years ago.

One particular stereotype of driving safety researchers is that we are somewhat risk averse since we deal with risk every day. Because of that, and because our data fluctuate and lives are on the line, we tend to be conservative in our thinking and writing. In general, therefore, we are not the best at getting information to you in a timely manner. Even when we are able to get the facts to you via an article or press release picked up by the media, the data may be presented in the wrong context or the main message we intended to convey wasn't there.

For example, when I was a young professor at the University of Idaho, my friend and very first graduate student, Jon Hankey, conducted a study with me that focused on fatigue when flying. (Jon is now the director of research and development for VTTI and had a huge role in getting our naturalistic driving data over the years.) This study looked at a pilot's ability to respond to an emergency situation after hours of mundane flight in a semi-sleep-deprived state. The pilots we recruited were kept awake for 24 hours. We then had them fly a simulator for two additional hours. It was an important study, revealing that pilots can recover pretty quickly and effectively when necessary. I was very excited, then, when the local paper came to do a story about our study. It was the first news article for my research. Jon and I talked to the reporter for about an hour, informing her of the merits and importance of our work.

At the very end of the discussion, the reporter said "Wow, it must have been hard on the pilots to fly that simulator after being up all night." To which I responded "Well, yes, it was a little bit of torture for them to get through it." The next day, with great anticipation, I stopped by a newspaper stand on the way to work. There was Jon and me with a caption that read "UI Professor puts sleepy pilots through 'torture.'" Of course, I was shocked and dismayed, thinking my young career would soon come to an abrupt end. In retrospect, however, we learned an important lesson and got a funny story out of it. To this day, Jon always prefers to delegate media interviews to our other researchers.

epy pilots through 'torture'

is capable of em off the as-

tributed more h is Hankey's gree in human blends engi- to create tech- ey will be the ree program, 1986. Another even students

st in pooped ny's military summer. He nt upon com- mer.

the project, UI College of ce designing e UI faculty. t link in the ngus. Boeing

TS back page

SHELLY GILDEHAUS PHOTO

RED-EYE FLIGHT: University of Idaho graduate student Jon Hankey (right) and UI psychology professor Tom Dingus have been studying tions of sleep-deprived pilots using a flight simulator.

But this story raises a bigger issue. Having done scores of interviews now over decades of work trying to get to you a clear message about how to drive safer, only a handful of those stories presented the message as clearly and correctly as I meant it to be delivered.

A second issue this industry experiences is that it is made up of both driving safety scientists and driving safety advocates. Although they certainly mean well, the advocates will "cherry pick" or exaggerate to advocate a point.

A recent example involved the following simple question: "What is a driver's risk associated with having a hands-free cell phone conversation while driving?" To answer this question, the advocates pointed to laboratory or survey data, saying that the risk was somewhere between driving while drunk and six times worse than driving while drunk. Media then picked up on this misinformation and perpetuated the story, creating inaccurate perceptions and muddying the waters of what driving safety scientists are really finding using actual on-road studies and crash data.

And what we have found is this: It only takes a few minutes to do a back-of-the-envelope calculation with real crash data to show that there is no way talking on a phone while driving has the same, or higher, risk as driving drunk. In 2014, people were having phone conversations almost 10% of the time while they were driving (http://www-nrd.nhtsa.dot.gov/Pubs/811184.pdf). If those drivers' risk was anywhere close to driving at the legal limit of alcohol, there would be a large, measurable increase in driving fatalities instead of the continued steady decline that we are experiencing.

Another issue with overemphasizing the dangers of cell phone conversations is that the basis of the comparison is terrible and may even have unintended consequences. If anything, this particular comparison minimizes the single biggest killer on our roadways: Driving drunk. If you drive drunk, you are drunk the entire trip. In addition, alcohol impairs judgment, leading to risky behaviors such as extreme speeding and choosing not to wear seat belts. However, if you're talking on your cell while driving, you can technically choose to pause or end the conversation at any time. Cell phone conversations do not lead to an increase in speeding or lack of seat belt use.

Media and politics being what they are, a related issue is that a complex problem usually becomes oversimplified. In other words, advocates want to bake our figurative cake and make the icing using a single ingredient. As we have seen, most crashes are extremely complicated. They involve multiple factors, or ingredients, *even for a single crash*. You can just imagine how complex things get trying to summarize thousands of crashes at the national database level.

I have a good advocate story from my history. In 2003, I got a call from a Washington Post reporter who was doing a story about an uptick in vehicle fatalities the previous year. An advocacy group called Public Citizen, which was founded by Ralph Nader, was advocating that the uptick was due to an increase in the number of SUVs on the road and the lack of a rollover safety standard for SUVs in general. It turns out that SUVs were classified as a "pickup truck" and did not have the same safety standards, such as roof crush standards, as other passenger cars. The advocacy group had a worthy goal and an argument with some merit.

The reporter asked me if I thought the increase in fatalities was due to the lack of an SUV rollover standard. I replied with something like: "The factors that are involved in the fatal crash rate are quite complex. This issue may be a factor, but it is getting more difficult to make the same level of progress in crashworthiness without adding significant cost or weight to a vehicle." What got left out of the story was my next thought: While rollover standards are important, we should also strive to continue making progress in active safety or crash avoidance technology.

What happened next was the fun part. Ralph Nader was quoted as essentially saying I was incorrigible and in the pocket of the car companies. Public Citizen wrote a letter to my employer suggesting that I was providing false statements and that I should be fired. None of this concerned me; in fact, I had the article framed and consider it a highlight of my career. But the important point is this: Advocates focus on one goal, they are great politicians, and they will go to great lengths to make their advocacy issue matter. However, unbiased, scientific views of the facts and complexities of the data involved in such issues are not necessarily a part of such groups' advocating. In this case, everything I said to the Washington Post reporter was correct, but I was "in the way" of the single ingredient that was being advocated. Ironically, I never disagreed with the merit of rollover standards for SUVs, I just didn't jump on the bandwagon and say that this was the one ingredient in the 2002 fatality rate increase.

These combined experiences are a big part of the motivation to write this book. My goal was to give you my best, most educated *opinion* based on what I have learned to date using on-road data and study findings. I have tried to make the information as clear and accurate as possible so that you can reduce and manage your risk while driving. Much of what is included in this book is grounded steadfastly in scientific fact, and some of it is on the cusp of being proven. Some of what you read is my opinion based on studying and thinking about driving safety for more than 30 years. The majority of information is based on driving data that come from drivers actually driving in a real-world setting, as opposed to laboratory or simulator studies. These real-world driving studies offer a clear advantage: At this point in time, crash risk can't be estimated from the lab.

Others will inevitably disagree with some aspects of this book, some will say I don't have sufficient data to give you a sound piece of advice, still others will misrepresent what I am trying to tell you by taking it out of context. A few will tell me about the great risk I have taken upon myself by giving people my opinions about driving safely. It's important to note, therefore, that:

1. I may be wrong, but I am probably not.

2. At least I tried when others have chosen to say we don't really know the answer about driving risks. I know we pretty much do have the answers.

3. I will update you through any means practical if I change my mind about what I presented, but there won't be too many updates.

4. Probably, and most importantly: Question everything you hear about driving safety in media reports, because a lot of it is inaccurate.

Thanks for reading. Remember to stay alert and sober, stay away from trucks, and KEEP YOUR EYES ON THE ROAD!

Tom and Mindy

CPSIA information can be obtained
at www.ICGtesting.com
Printed in the USA
LVOW01s1321090116

469543LV00021B/182/P